LEADSOLOGY®
THE SCIENCE OF BEING
IN DEMAND

An Ethically Cunning Lead Generation Model for Coaches,

Consultants, Advisors, Trainers and Teachers,

and Those Offering Services

TOM
POLAND

DEDICATION

The book is dedicated to my wife and soul mate, Ute Strenger.

Thank you for the many growth opportunities that you have so elegantly and generously gifted me.

I will remain eternally grateful for your seemingly endless patience, your seriously wicked sense of humour, and your astute and intuitive insights.

Thank you for you. I like me better when you're with me.

And hot damn, you're pretty!

Kuss kuss.

Tom Poland
Chief Leadsologist
January 17th 2016

LEADSOLOGY® RESOURCES

With Leadsology® you benefit on two levels when you engage with our community.

For example, when you join the Leadsology® Facebook group you'll not only benefit from the new client generating tips, strategies and free events but you also get to see exactly how I attract new clients, members and followers. You also can "swipe and deploy" everything that you see me do and install those practices into your own business for great personal benefit.

Here are five ways to benefit from Leadsology®

1. Go to **www.facebook.com/groups/leadsology/** and begin to benefit from regular advice on how to generate inbound new client inquiries as well as enjoying invitations to exclusive, free events. Just log into your Facebook account, search for Leadsology® and send me a request to join the group. It's completely free and your lead generation capability will be enhanced enormously.

2. Download the free, full-color, one-page Leadsology® Model to print out so that you can see at a glance all the key elements that create a truly powerful lead generation system. Go to **www.leadsology.guru/the-model/** and get your free copy now.

3. Take our unique Leadsology® Diagnostic Assessment. You'll answer some carefully chosen questions and then we'll send you a fully customized report showing you how much your revenue would increase once you implement the recommendations in this book and even more in-depth recommendations for each part of your lead generation model. The Leadsology® Diagnostic Assessment is completely free. Go to **www.leadsology.guru/ diagnostic/** to get your personalized Leadsology® Recommendations Report.

4. Join thousands of others who've benefited from my strategies by enrolling in the internationally acclaimed 8-week Leadsology® Program and I'll walk with you, step-by-step, hand-in-digital-hand, as you bring Leadsology® to life in YOUR business. You'll soon be enjoying the security and satisfaction of having a stream of high quality, inbound, new client enquiries flowing into your business virtually every week of the year. Go to **www.leadsology.guru/program/** to find out more.

5. Finally, if you're not sure if the Leadsology® Program is right for you, and you'd like to find out then you can go to www.Book-AChatWithTom.com and find a time for us to talk online. This is NOT a sales call and it's NOT a coaching call, it's simply to see if what I have is a fit for your needs.

PRAISE FOR LEADSOLOGY®
THE SCIENCE
OF BEING IN DEMAND

THIS BOOK WILL BE IN DEMAND TOO

A terrific book. With trademark clarity and honesty, Tom Poland shows how trainers, consultants, and other advisers can generate a reliable flow of high quality leads. It's a really excellent method, and presented with verve and wit.

Richard Koch
Author of The 80/20 Principle which sold over one million copies

ONE OF THE BEST BOOKS ON MARKETING EVER WRITTEN

Tom Poland is not only an expert marketer but a master teacher. Step-by-step instructions are easy to follow and you can build a complete marketing system without needing to be a genius. More practical and actionable than the 4-year marketing degree I completed.

Richard Petrie
Speed Marketing

FABULOUS!

Leadsology® gives you the science behind figuring out EXACTLY how to create demand and generate a flow of high quality leads. Buy this book and put the formula to work in your business - the results speak for themselves.

Dr Ivan Misner
Founder Business Network International (BNI) and
New York Times best selling author

EASILY ONE OF THE MOST VALUABLE BUSINESS BOOKS I'VE READ

By this point I must have read over 400 books on marketing, sales and business and I can honestly say I found this one of the most valuable.

So much useful stuff in Tom's book; it's accessible and Tom is a charming, down-to-earth guide, but the methodology is rigorous too. It's never dumbed down or over-simplified, because there is a lot to the Leadsology® model.

Tom's model gives you not only a ton of useful ideas, but the overarching framework you need to fit them together. It's a complete system, and it gives you clarity.

Rob Tyson
The Tyson Report

A BOOK DEFINITELY WORTH BUYING

Business books that you don't want to put down are very rare, but Tom Poland's "Leadsology®" is one of them. Tom Poland goes right to the heart of lead generation this wonderful book, which is full of real world wisdom.

As the author of 47 books, I hate having to say that I wish I had written this one! It has certainly given me loads of ideas for improving my next book.

If I ever get chance, I will invite Tom Poland to address my MBA students in one of the world's top Business Schools. They really need to know and understand material like this.

Professor Malcolm McDonald MA(Oxon) MSc PhD DLitt DSc
Emeritus Professor, Cranfield University School of Management
Author of Marketing Plans which sold over 500,000 copies

A MUST-READ BOOK

Brilliant! Leadsology® lays out a step-by-step process for advisors who want to create a cut-through marketing message and get the message out to the marketplace so that inbound new client enquiries flow in like turning on a tap.

In particular, I recommend searching the book for "The Waterfall", "The Dinner Party Question", and "The Value Slider" which are all original and brilliant concepts that the author has introduced. As a successful consultant for over a decade, I recognize marketing gold when I see it.

Ari Galper
Author of Unlock The Game

DON'T THINK ABOUT IT, GRAB THIS BOOK NOW AND BREAK DOWN THE BARRIERS HOLDING YOUR BUSINESS BACK!

Tom Poland's book is a great resource that lays out common entrepreneur pitfalls for coaches, consultants, advisors, and experts. He then goes on to provide solutions to these problems that slow people from making the progress they desire to run a successful business -- ultimately enabling them to live an impactful life.

The author's decades of experience are evident is his rich understanding of the topics, along with his insightful delivery. Don't think about it, grab this book now and breakdown the barriers holding your business back!

Charles Byrd
Evernote Productivity Guru

PUT THIS BOOK INTO PRACTICE THEN STEP BACK AND WATCH YOUR WHOLE WORLD CHANGE

If you're an advisor, coach, consultant, or trainer, who's tried a lot of techniques and spent a lot of time and money on marketing with mixed-to-awful results, I strongly urge you to open the Kindle version of this book and search for "Here's why the traditional Product Funnel probably won't work for you."

In coaching business owners from start-up through $100M mark, I've seen more service-based companies waste more time, money, and energy on marketing funnels than you would even believe. In SO many cases, it's all been a waste. This is particularly true for business owners who try to mimic info-marketing models.

The author explains not only why this doesn't work, but also how to evaluate your marketing efforts, explains how to properly define your ideal client, step-by-step instructions for crafting an effective message, advises on selecting the effective media, and a number of other critical topics.

If you read and implement what the author suggests in this book you'll have done what 95% of marketers have NOT done; you'll have made

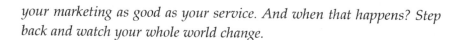

your marketing as good as your service. And when that happens? Step back and watch your whole world change.

Robert Michon
The Unstoppable CEO

SPECIFICALLY FOR COACHES & CONSULTANTS

If you're a coach or consultant who wants more leads, this book is a must read because it's specifically for you.

I've been studying and using direct response marketing since 1997 and this is a great resource to now add to my tool chest!

Kevin Thompson
Marketer, consultant, coach

HELPFUL FOR MY START UP BUSINESS

I am planning to start my own business and I still have some questions when it comes to finding the right clients for me and how my marketing model should be. Leadsology® has helped me to understand a lot of things especially on the first chapter about the revenue and the profit and how it should be enough for my chosen lifestyle. This is a really good book to read for people like me who wants to start their own business. It is packed with resources and useful tips that you can actually implement.

Alexandra Karenina Arabelo

HOLDS A MIRROR UP TO YOUR MARKETING - AND SHOWS YOU WHERE IT'S UGLY. (THAT'S A GOOD THING)

Tom Poland is clearly gifted at creating a simple-to-understand framework for what it takes to generate leads for your business. I consider myself a marketing professional, and reading through Tom's book gave me good ideas and showed a few places I could improve.

If yu're struggling to generate leads in your service business, this book will help you solve that problem.

Frank Bria
Author, Speaker, Strategist

GREAT MARKETING BOOK FOR SERVICE PROFESSIONALS

This book is a tool chest of easy to use strategies to attract good numbers of high quality clients.

Every chapter has some nuggets of wisdom that are easy to use. Highly recommended.

Graham McGregor
Marketing and sales consultant, trainer, coach

A HIGHLY ACTIONABLE BOOK THAT HELPS YOU CREATE A STRATEGY TO INCREASE LEADS INTO YOUR BUSINESS

I absolutely loved this book. Tom delivers so many practical tips for creating a lead machine. One of my favorites parts of the book is when he goes into the mistakes that we make when we set out to increase our leads. Mistake #12 really hit home which is lowering prices to increase leads. This was a good reminder that the race to the bottom is not the way to create a lead generating machine and in some cases raising prices actually helps increase lead flow. I highly recommend it to any business owner in need of leads!

Joshua Millage
Entrepreneur and co-founder of Lifter LMS

PRACTICAL AND EFFECTIVE LEAD GENERATION SYSTEM

Leadsology® is a practical, effective and implementable system that helps you create a predictable flow of high quality inbound new client enquiries into your business. Tom's book and system will show you how to stop random acts of marketing and get you back in the driver's seat running your business. You can easily swipe and deploy his 10-step lead generation model so that you can work smart not harder.

This is a great book for advisors and consultants to learn how to create a system that brings in a predictable flow of clients and shows you how best to invest your marketing time. I have had the privilege of working with the author and have been so pleased with the results and the practical, effective and easy to implement nature of this model which is all laid out in the book. I definitely recommend this book.

Susan Kleinschmidt
Consultant, Trainer Coach

COOL NEW LEAD GENERATION ROADMAP FOR SERVICE AND ADVISORY PROFESSIONALS

Not to toot my own horn, but I've been an internationally recognized expert on Sales, Lead Generation and Positioning for many years now, so I know a thing or two about great lead generation systems.

There are tons of books out there about lead gen, but what's different with this book is that it's especially written for folks who specialize in service and/ or advisory businesses, and NOT for those who sell physical products.

They say that specificity is power and I believe that the advisor-specific strategies in this book are what makes it so powerful. Tom's book truly "dis-

rupts" the status quo, and offers a road map that will lead you to generate a consistent flow of high quality, inbound leads.

Buy this book. Implement every suggestion. Then sit back and watch the new clients flow into your business.

Erik Luhrs
GURU Selling System

AN INSIGHTFUL RESOURCE!

In Leadsology®, Tom Poland offers advisors, coaches, consultants, and trainers a step-by-step Lead Generation Model – one that is beautifully tailored to this audience's specific needs. Grounded in professional experience and observations, Leadsology is written with passion and deep knowledge.

An insightful, elegant, and practical resource – I certainly recommend it.

Dorie Clark
Marketing, Branding and Management Consultant

PAVING THE ROAD TO SUCCESS

For coaches, trainers and consultants like me it is often challenging to balance delivery and marketing, to find new clients while servicing established ones, to have such a finely tuned business model in place that it creates ongoing high quality enquiries.

The comprehensive ten-step Leadsology® model outlined in this book helped me to get clear about the what, the where, the when and the how. The structure, the suggestions and guidelines, they all make sense.

With over 35 years of experience, Tom knows what he is talking about. His clarity and wisdom shine through every story, every comprehensive model and concept that are clearly only so simple because Tom has done all the work.

I also really appreciate the honesty and candor with which he points out likely pitfalls, especially poignant when they are the ones I already fell into. If you want to grow your business and have a good life to boost, read this book - and then work with Tom.

Angela Heise
Trainer, consultant, coach

FINALLY!

For anyone who like me is an advisor (or coach or consultant or trainer) and has done the run-around trying to find a genuine specialist in how to message and market our types of service, this is the ultimate answer: Leadsology® is genuinely tailored to us, with tremendous insight that is completely on the mark about us, presented as a simple, proven, step-by-step progressive process you are walked through, hand-in-hand, by a true expert. And it works!

Elizabeth Brown
Branding and Marketing Consultant

A TREASURE TROVE OF INFORMATION

Leadsology® – The Science of Being in Demand is a treasure trove of information not only about lead generation, but also about how to wire our whole business for success. Tom Poland's 10-part model for being in demand is a comprehensive summary of all the elements we need to have optimized for our business to be coasting along like a well-oiled wheel.

There are so many gems of information in this book, that if we even take one, and implement it, it makes a difference. I know that I've already changed my marketing message because of this, and people are much more interested in what I do now. There is also a surprising departure from the normal way of structuring online marketing – specifically for what Tom calls "advisors". This is vital information that could be the one thing that brings advisors the revenues and number of clients we are really looking for.

Glenda Nicholls
Founder, Money Success System

LEAD GENERATION: NOW A SIMPLE AND ELEGANT SCIENCE

Many of us employ a very hit and miss approach to marketing and lead generation – with very hit and miss results. With "Leadsology®" however, Tom Poland has turned lead generation into a science that is both simple and elegant.

In a market where we've all got used to the same old marketing formulae, Tom brings a fresh approach that provides cut through in a noisy world. You'll enjoy the easy-to-implement, step-by-step approach outlined in this book.

And, I havee no doubt, you'll enjoy the results this unique system can generate.

Dawn Russell
Founder of Heartwired, trainer and coach

CONTENTS

✺ ✺ ✺

PREFACE

WHY THIS BOOK

THE FIRST REASON why I wrote this book is that it simply doesn't exist.

What I mean by that is that there is no single book, that I am aware of, that specifically lays out a <u>proven</u>, <u>step-by-step</u> Lead Generation Model for Coaches, Consultants, Advisors, Teachers and Trainers and others who offer a Service. (For the sake of simplicity throughout this book I'll refer to these professionals as "Advisors").

Sure, there are plenty of books on marketing, sales and Lead Generation, but none of them addresses the subject specifically for Advisors.

And the reason that addressing the subject of Lead Generation specifically for Advisors is so important is that much of the generic marketing and sales methods which are taught simply don't work for Advisors.

For example, what works for retailers or manufacturers very often does not work for Advisors who essentially make a living from their ideas, rather than with a physical product.

Therefore, any book which addresses the subject of Marketing and Lead Generation in general terms is likely to be worse than useless for Advisors, because it will have them undertaking all sorts of marketing activity which is not specifically customised for those offering a service or advice, and thereby has them wasting time, energy and money with little or no result to show for it.

The second reason for writing this book is that it's in me. What I mean by that is this: At the time of writing, I've spent 35 years in sales and marketing. That's 35 years of learning about Lead Generation, 35 years of observing Lead Generation, 35 years of doing Lead Generation and, for the last eight years, I've taught Lead Generation professionally and full-time.

It's said that good teachers will faithfully teach what they have been taught, but that great teachers will teach what they have observed. At the risk of appearing just a tad arrogant, I like to think that in my own modest way I've made some fresh observations about Lead Generation over those 35 years. So I guess you could say that, for me, writing this book is like giving birth. It's a natural consequence of having "incubated" Lead Generation strategies and tactics for the thick end of four decades. Like a newborn baby, eventually it just had to come out, at times kicking and screaming.

Reason number three is that I want to leave the world a better place. As you'll discover in Part One, effective Lead Generation transforms lives, businesses and organisations, families, communities and, indeed, whole states, territories and countries.

Lead Generation is the number one essential skill for creating fresh cash flow, and thereby in turn creating lifestyle transformations including the funding of better educational opportunities, better medical care, more choice in housing location and quality, holidays and also the funding of philanthropic or charitable pursuits.

They say that nothing happens in the world until something is sold, but the fact is that nothing gets sold until an enquiry (a lead) is generated. This book reveals a step-by-step model that increases demand for the services of Advisors and just as importantly, it also pulls back the curtain on what does not work in respect to ramping up demand for an Advisor.

Finally, a potentially damaging admission, but one that will benefit you significantly: a well-written and well-targeted book is, in itself, a great lead generator. To illustrate this point, you can refer to the bookmark that came with this book, or indeed visit us at www.leadsology.guru and look for our current totally irresistible offer.

When you take advantage of that offer, I will have … ta daaaa … generated a lead. (In fact, the very fact that you bought this book means I've already generated a lead ☺)

So there you have it — a clearly stated and open disclosure of the most selfish of these four reasons: like you, I like to enjoy the benefits of generating leads. You are welcome to "swipe and deploy" the idea of writing a book to generate leads. More on that In Part Three, Chapter Four.

THE LEADSOLOGY® STORY

Following on from the subject of why I wrote this book there is actually a deeper question to be answered, which is how the Leadsology® concept came about in the very first place and why, in addition to writing a Leadsology® book, I have I created a Leadsology® webinar, a Leadsology® Facebook group, a Leadsology® program and why, at every opportunity I get, I speak about Leadsology® at conferences, workshops and seminars. And there are two main reasons.

Reason #1

I created the Leadsology® concept first and foremost because of the absolute transformation that occurs in the life of an Advisor when they create a *system* (keyword) that brings in a predictable flow of high-quality, inbound new client enquiries into their business.

Until such a system is embedded into a business the owner's future, prosperity is precarious to say the least. It's different if you are an employee in a big corporation, because your paycheck is your security. However, for a business owner, security lies in your ability to bring in new clients on a regular basis, if not daily then at least weekly.

But I'm not just talking about the potential impact of Leadsology® on a business owner.

Leadsology® is like throwing a stone into a pond; a ripple effect emanates from where the stone lands, and in our metaphor, the ripples include the quality of life of the business owner's family, increased security for employees and suppliers, and of course the positive effect on local communities when each of these groups of stakeholders benefit from a business that keeps growing.

In my mind, Leadsology® is about the fulfilment of my life purpose because of the positive impact it has on the lives of all who benefit from it.

Reason #2 and the Story Of Leadsology®

This reason may surprise you, but it explains the origins of Leadsology® and why it was born out of feelings of underwhelm, disappointment and frustration. I'll explain.

In between owning my own businesses, I had a period of several years working in a senior management role for a large international corporation. It was a very satisfying period of time. However the day came when I knew that, in order to fulfil my particular destiny, I needed to jump the job track and start up my own business again.

And so in 1995 I launched the Entrepreneur's Success Program, which went on to positively impact the lives of thousands of business owners across Australia and New Zealand.

However, the early days were tough because I had a big obstacle to overcome — how to create a regular flow of new client enquiries.

I should hasten to add that most Advisors not only suffer from the same hurdle, but they have the additional challenge of finally discovering what they need to do in order to create an effective lead generation machine, but failing to implement.

Maybe you've noticed that ☺?

If you are like so many of my new clients, you probably face the same distinct lead generation obstacles: knowledge and implementation.

The first of these two obstacles was not really a problem for me because I had been fortunate enough to have graduated from Brian Tracy's Phoenix seminar in 1989, some six years prior. It was a terrific experience not just in personal development, but also in the creation of a mindset to get things done. Brian Tracy said that there were four things I needed to do in order to accelerate the achievement of my goals:

1. Hire a proven, effective mentor.

2. Pay them as much money as I possibly could, because he said if you get a free mentor then you won't feel obligated to execute his/her advice, and the mentor wouldn't feel committed to keep giving you advice for more than a few weeks.

3. Sit down with my mentor and figure out my objectives, strategy and actions.

4. Rinse and repeat by creating weekly accountability meetings where my actions and results were reviewed and where I could also receive more guidance.

By following the above advice, I became a very good implementer.

But the first problem still remained, which was that of figuring out exactly what I needed to implement in order to create a proven system for lead generation.

As an avid consumer of information, I bought an incalculable number of books (and read them!), attended a similar number of seminars and workshops in various countries, all the while making notes on key points and action items which I then ticked off my rather long list.

In short, I learned and implemented like crazy.

It was like a continual and seemingly never-ending cycle of discovery, development and unfortunately, massive disappointment ,because everything that I had learned from the feet of so many marketing masters failed to make any significant difference whatsoever in my results.

Hence my underwhelm, disappointment and frustration.

When I relate the above story to audiences and ask them to raise their hand if they have had a similar experience, almost everyone immediately thrusts an arm into the air.

I find this to be absolutely staggering! That so many people, probably millions the world over, have spent so much money, time and energy in learning from supposed gurus, only to discover that what was being taught was, to put it frankly, worse than useless.

It was during this time of bewilderment that I was attending a seminar and the speaker said something that I've never forgotten some 21 years later. I can't remember the name of the speaker ,but what he said was this: *"good teachers teach what they have been taught; great teachers teach what they have observed"*.

It hit me like a lightning bolt: all the teachers I had been learning from work at teaching what they had been taught without actually observing reality for themselves. Doubtless they had been to various seminars and workshops and read various books like I had. But my conclusion was that they never actually contextualised what they had learned to specific marketplaces (e.g. professional services), or what they were teaching was out of date and no longer worked. Either way, the result was the same — they were wasting their clients' time and money.

It was then that I set out on my Leadsology® journey by throwing out the marketing rulebook, starting afresh and testing and measuring everything. And making a lot, a lot, a lot of mistakes.

And that experience is why Leadsology® exists today.

After some 21 years of continual testing, refining, experimenting, trialing, and measuring, the Leadsology® system is ready for release so that the years of wasted time, money, and energy on ineffective marketing advice can finally be over.

Finally, Leadsology® is ready for the world. Hopefully you're ready for it.

MY CREDENTIALS

I've mentioned that I've been involved in sales and marketing for over 35 years, so I guess that's a significant part of my credentials.

However, in and of itself, that is not especially significant compared with the results that I've personally achieved in various businesses of my own, as well as the results I've achieved in helping over 2,000 business owners across 193 different industries from all around the world.

I started my first business at age 24 and I have gone on to start and sell four others, taking two of them International. In that time, I've managed teams of over 100 people and annual revenue of more than $20 million. The Leadsology® model that I reveal in this book has generated many millions of dollars for my own businesses and for those of my clients.

To reference the latter claim, I invite you to go to **www.leadsology.guru** and check out the "Client Results" tab.

There are probably plenty of other people who have spent the thick end of four decades in sales and marketing, but I haven't seen many that are being credited by their clients with generating multiple millions in extra revenue.

That's why I don't regard my 35 years of experience as being enough to establish my credentials; it's got to be all about results.

It may also be true that I have a gram of entrepreneurial spirit in me which could also further serve to enhance my credibility. In addition to the above-mentioned businesses, I currently have significant interests and active involvement in three distinctly separate and different businesses, and I use much, if not all, of the 10 Step In Demand Model revealed in Part Three in each of these businesses. So I like to think that I'm walking the talk.

It may also give you some measure of confidence to know that my work has been reprinted physically in 27 countries and that I've shared international speaking platforms with the likes of Michael Gerber of E-Myth fame, Brian Tracy of Brian Tracy International, Richard Koch, who is the author of which sold over one million copies, Michael Port and many others.

Lastly, I operate a "Hype-Free" zone whereby I am 100 percent committed to giving you, my valued reader, only the strategies, tactics and *methods* that have been proven in the real world to increase demand for your services.

Hopefully the above will reassure you that this book is worth reading, and even more, that it's worth implementing.

WHO WILL BENEFIT FROM THIS BOOK

Much of the information in this book, and especially in Parts Two and Three, will benefit any business, organisation or solopreneur. However, as mentioned previously, I've written this book specifically for Coaches, Consultants, Advisors, Teachers and Trainers, and anyone else who offers a Service.

You will benefit greatly from this book if you possess a strong determination to set up Leadsology® systems that will keep your Pipeline full of fresh, inbound, highly qualified leads and enquiries.

If that sounds like you, then please be warned that achieving this objective is neither simple nor easy unless you have the know-how. In that regard, think of it as being a bit like trying to crack open a highly secure safe. It's neither simple nor easy until you have the combination. Leadsology® "cracks that code" and gives you the precise combination for setting up Lead Generation systems so that you can continually and confidently grow your revenue.

Also of great importance, Leadsology® introduces you to the concept of Scalability (Part Three, Chapter 9 especially covers this) so that you can not only grow your revenue to multiple six and seven figures, but also comfortably achieve the lifestyle of your dreams in 30-40 hours per week.

The Scope of This Book

As mentioned previously, this book gives Advisors a proven step-by-step model for ramping up demand and generating a high-quality flow of inbound lead enquiries. I reveal absolutely everything you need to know to systematically and predictably generate those leads so that you never have to worry again about where your next client is coming from.

The key word in the previous paragraph is "systematically". Gone will be the days of random and desperate marketing activity where you wish, hope and pray that a prospect will make an enquiry, or that an enquiry will convert into a client.

You will, perhaps for the first time, feel that you are "Master and Commander" of your own destiny because you'll be able to relax in the confidence that you are the owner of a business that operates like a conveyor belt, predictably and systematically producing a flow of inbound lead enquiries.

As also mentioned above, this book doesn't stop there. I further reveal how to deliver value to your clients in much less time, for much more money, and with much more enjoyment (you'll achieve this by avoiding the mistakes I outline in Part Two and by implementing the Leadsology® Model that I reveal in Part Three).

Note that I use the terms "Lead Generation" and "Being in Demand" and "In Demand" interchangeably throughout this book, all of which come about once you implement Leadsology®. Effectively, they all refer to the same thing, which is to generate high-quality, inbound, fresh enquiries to your business from people or organisations who represent your absolute Ideal Client. More on the latter in Part Three, Chapter Two.

A NOTE ON MY USE OF TITLE CASE

In this book I display in Title Case words that describe a term or concept that is especially important. For example, I do this when I refer to your Marketing Message or your Value Proposition or Being In Demand. I appreciate that this may not be the technically correct use of Title Case. However, I want to flag for you those terms and concepts which require extra attention.

PART ONE

WHY BEING IN DEMAND
IS IN DEMAND

BEING IN DEMAND

SAM'S PROBLEM — AND MAYBE YOURS TOO?

SAM IS A brilliant consultant. He's a genius at re-engineering software systems and providing training during a merger and integration process. Sam's problem, however, is that he has a "10 service" trapped in "2 marketing".

In other words, while Sam is brilliant at what he does and while the few clients that he's worked with absolutely love his work, he has no effective Lead Generation systems in place, and therefore he is simply not In Demand.

Sam relies purely on Word-Of-Mouth Marketing, which means that he has absolutely zero control over the number of enquiries flowing into his business. As a result, Sam's life is the living personification of the term "feast or famine".

At times, Sam's anxiety levels are extreme and that in turn results in dysfunctional reactions such as panic attacks, escaping into alcohol, other acts of overindulgence including shopping sprees, eating too much, and other dysfunctions such as *"going home when*

I'm tired of being nice to people".

When work dries up, he engages in random acts of marketing and the prospects that he approaches are turned off by what they perceive as his *"dance of the desperate "*.

At the heart of Sam's problem is his failure to dedicate a specific block of time for Lead Generation.

This means his revenue and workflow are like a rollercoaster. At the top of the rollercoaster ride, Sam's got plenty of client work and cash flow, but no spare time to enjoy it.

And at the bottom of the rollercoaster, Sam's got plenty of spare time, but no money to enjoy it.

Either way, Sam suffers from numerous "lack of demand" symptoms that we'll explore below.

For Pam, on the other hand, life is good. Many years ago she adopted one of my core recommendations and changed her calendar from the Roman Calendar system to the Poland Calendar system.

A work week in the Roman calendar looks like this: Monday, Tuesday, Wednesday, Thursday, Friday.

By contrast, a work week in the Poland Calendar system looks like this: Monday, Tuesday, Marketing Day, Thursday, Friday.

Did you spot the difference? I'm sure you did: I recommend that, like Pam, you dedicate one whole day to doing nothing else but focusing on Lead Generation.

And because Pam created the weekly Marketing Day habit, and because she implemented many of my other Leadsology® recommendations, she can relax because she's created a predictable, controllable flow of high-quality, fresh, inbound new client enquiries almost every single week of the year, including those weeks when she is enjoying holidays and overseas travel.

Both of the above examples are true stories. The first is typical of Advisors who rely on Word-Of-Mouth Marketing for Lead Generation.

The second example is typical of Advisors who create Leadsology® systems. The good news is that by reading this book you get to choose which of those two stories you want your life to look like.

YOUR REVENUE PROBLEM AND THE SOLUTION

To benefit from my Leadsology® model, it's critical for you to understand the nature of the problem of lack of demand, the symptoms of the problem, and also the causes of the problem.

Let's start with the problem itself.

A lack of demand results in lack of revenue, so we need to view the problem primarily in terms of a lack of revenue.

A problem is classically defined as the gap between what you have and what you want.

For example, if you have monthly sales revenue of $20,000, but need monthly sales revenue of $30,000 to support your desired lifestyle, then your problem can be identified as $10,000 — that number being the difference between what you've got and what you want. Your business might add a zero or two onto the above example, but the principle is the same: there is a gap between what you have and what you want.

I invite you to identify both the size of your problem and the solution by completing the following (note that I have inserted an example in brackets at the end of each line):

A. My current monthly sales revenue is: $ _____ ($20,000)

B. The monthly sales revenue I need to support my lifestyle: $ _____ ($30,000)

C. The difference (B minus A): $ _____ ($10,000)

D. Average sales revenue per month from one sale: $_____ ($2,000)

E. The number of new sales I need each month (C divide D): _____ (5)

F. Conversion percentage from qualified prospect to a sale: _____ percent (50 percent)

G. Number of new leads I need each month (E divide F): _____ (10)

THE LAST NUMBER IS THE MOST CRITICAL NUMBER IN YOUR LIFE

It's what I call your "#1 Number," because it is metaphorically the key to unlocking the door to a highly desirable future.

Your answer for row G needs to be not only your #1 Number but also your #1 objective in life. The reason is probably self-evident.

However, at the risk of stating the bleeding obvious, if you get enough high-quality leads flowing into your business, then you generate the revenue you need to support a highly desirable personal lifestyle, which may include providing top quality education for your children, medical care for loved ones, living daily in your dream home in your dream location, and funding sports, hobbies and charitable interests, and local or overseas holidays.

To paraphrase Neil Armstrong, the first man to walk on the moon, *"that's one small number for you, but one giant leap for your lifestyle "*.

The Primary Cause of Lack of Revenue

Most people believe that there are three primary causes of lack of revenue; however, in the vast majority of cases, I'd suggest there's really only one cause.

Mark Twain said *"It's not what we don't know that hurts us, it's the things that we think we know that just ain't so "*.

Another way of expressing this might be that if we incorrectly identify the cause of the problem of lack of revenue, then it's very likely we will waste time, energy, and possibly money trying to fix something that simply isn't broken.

The three most commonly identified causes for lack of demand are the following:

1. A problem with Lead Generation

2. A problem with Lead Conversion (converting leads into clients)

3. A problem with Value Delivery (client work or service delivery that is not effective enough to generate referrals, and is therefore a missed opportunity in contributing to revenue growth)

To correctly identify the *primary* cause of lack of revenue/lack of demand, I need you to answer a couple of questions.

Question One: what percentage of clients have been happy with your work?

Question Two: what percentage of qualified prospects do you convert into clients once you are in front of them? Note that a qualified prospect is defined here as people who are aware of their need for what you have, have the money to pay you, and arrive when the timing is perfect.

If your answer to Question One was 80 percent or more, then clearly the primary cause of your revenue problem is not poor quality service or advice. So my strong recommendation is that you quit even thinking about messing with it.

If your clients genuinely feel that your service is more than good enough, then your service is more than good enough. Leave it alone and eliminate Value Delivery from your thoughts as a primary cause of your lack-of-demand problem.

If your answer to Question Two was 50 percent or more, then your problem is not Lead Conversion (otherwise known as "sales" or "selling").

A marketing research association that I studied with many years ago stated that top salespeople will convert 50 percent of qualified prospects immediately; 25 percent will be converted later and the remaining 25 percent will either go somewhere else or will never buy. Therefore, if you're batting at 50 percent or more, then Lead Conversion also is not the primary cause of your problem.

We have therefore most likely eliminated both Lead Conversion and Value Delivery as the primary cause of your problem of lack of revenue, and so we are left with Lead Generation as the primary culprit.

Which is correct in approximately 97 percent of cases.

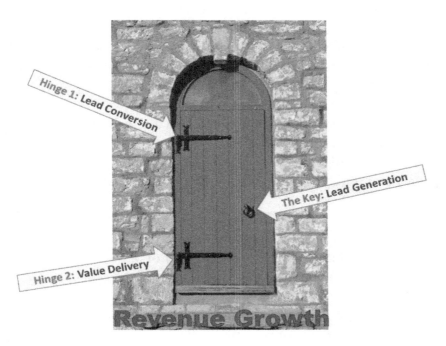

That's not to say that both Lead Conversion and Value Delivery are unimportant. On the contrary, they are critical.

But here is how I see Lead Conversion and Value Delivery relating to Lead Generation.

Imagine a massive brick wall with a door in the middle of it. And imagine that on the other side of that door lies significant and continually increasing revenue growth, plus all the lifestyle transformations that the extra cash flow will bring.

Now imagine that the door has two hinges and one keyhole with a key in it. In this metaphor, we can label one hinge "Lead Conversion" and the second hinge "Value Delivery". And the key in the keyhole can be labelled "Lead Generation".

In other words, you need effective Lead Conversion and Value Delivery systems so that the door will smoothly swing open when unlocked.

However, no matter how strong those two hinges are, the door is never going to open without the key. The best sales process in the world and the highest-quality service in the world are both completely and utterly useless without a flow of new leads to convert and deliver value to.

In summary, so far we've identified the size of your revenue problem and the solution, which is the number of new leads that you need each week in order to meet your revenue objectives.

We've also identified a lack of Lead Generation as being the number one primary cause of your problem.

And that's what this book will give you: Leadsology® is the master key to Lead Generation, which in turn leads to a predictable, controllable flow of high-quality, inbound leads, which in turn generate new clients and fresh revenue, which in turn gives you the lifestyle you desire for yourself and your loved ones.

THE SEVEN PRIMARY SYMPTOMS OF LACK OF REVENUE

Having defined the size of your problem (row C above) and identified the solution (row G above) plus the primary cause, let's now look at some of the symptoms of the problem.

It's important to do this because the symptoms can be turned into motivational reasons that will fuel your determination to implement Leadsology® and thereby become In Demand.

SYMPTOM #1 IS ANXIETY. Sleepless nights spent worrying about where the money is going to come from to pay the bills. Stress-filled days trying to figure out how to generate some leads. Anxious moments worrying about whether a prospective new client will go ahead. Relationship tension as your wife/husband/partner/parent expresses concern about mortgage or rent payments. Embarrassment at the supermarket when your card payment is declined. Tense minutes scratching around for a dollar here and a dollar there in order to fill your car with a little petrol. Worry as you look at the ever-increasing pile of unpaid bills on your desk. Actually, many of my clients don't have distress around getting new business or paying bills, but they do have a more positive form of stress called eustress (Google it!) that motivates them to continually strive for higher levels of performance. Whichever form of stress you are experiencing, you can use it to fuel your motivation tanks.

SYMPTOM #2 IS RESTRICTED CHOICES. This is where you experience significant limitations in where you live, the type of house or apartment you choose, compromises in medical and health care, lower-quality educational opportunities for children, lower-quality holidays and fewer of them, inability to financially support a loved one or a charity of choice, less choice around indulging in your favourite hobbies or sports or pastimes, having to put up with inferior and less-efficient/effective technology at work, and pretty much everything else you can think of that requires cash.

SYMPTOM #3 IS THE LOSS OF SELF-ESTEEM. This is rarely spoken about, but in quiet moments people have mentioned this to me. Someone who is not In Demand often feels, rightly or wrongly, that they suffer from an erosion of respect from their wife/husband/partner/parents because they are living at a level which is far below their potential as a provider. This perception of a loss of respect from others triggers a loss of self-respect. There is no doubt in my mind that this is a tragedy of epic proportions, because we're talking about a person's inability to fulfil their role as a provider and, indeed, were also talking about nothing less than their inability to fulfil their life potential.

While, the above symptoms may seem somewhat depressing, but the good news is that pain is fuel. In other words, the more you can relate to the above symptoms, the more motivated you are likely to be to take the creation of Lead Generation systems seriously.

Nothing short of a 100 percent commitment to Being In Demand will get you over the line.

So if revenue is not at the levels that you would like it to be, then rather than feeling depressed, use the pain and disappointment that you have felt as fuel to move forward. As someone once said, *"reasons are the fuel in the furnace of motivation "*.

We could rightly describe the above as "pain-based" symptoms. The following are what I would call "desire-based" symptoms that can be used to equal effect as motivators for developing Lead Generation systems that have your services In Demand. This is particularly true if you're comfortable with your revenue levels but you still have a burning desire to achieve more.

Symptom #4 is resentment. The symptom can probably be fairly described as a mixture of both pain and desire. A lot of people tell me that they want to do better in terms of Being In Demand because they see others with a lower-quality service doing better in the marketplace and that really annoys them. So they experience *resentment* because they see themselves as seemingly the world's best-kept secret, and they also feel the *desire* to do better than others peddling poorer-quality services.

Symptom #5 is a knowing. What I mean by "a knowing" is that for many people there is a knowledge, or a deep belief, that they can do better, and that indeed they feel they must do better. However we articulate this knowledge, the fact remains that there is a deep-seated awareness that you can play the game of business at a much higher level. I use the word "can" in the sense that the capacity is in you, but you just have to figure out a way to release it. It's a matter of stepping into your destiny and fulfilling your Life Purpose starting with Being in Demand through effective Lead Generation. Leadsology® will show you how to do that.

Symptom #6 is taking on clients that are not a fit. When revenue and cash flow are tight, it's incredibly tempting to take on a client that is not quite the right fit for your services. We have all done it and we have all lived to regret it.

For example, my forte is working with professional advisors. But 10 years ago I was still taking on board retailers and manufacturers, not necessarily because I was short of cash flow, but more because I found it difficult to pass up an opportunity. Yes, I managed to keep my clients happy and they benefited from a modicum of results, but I never felt comfortable about going into client meetings.

And it's not just the client-to-Advisor fit; it is also the service -to-Advisor fit. For example, a specialist productivity consultant might be tempted by a project that called for recruitment expertise. While there might be some crossover, a specialist in the latter service is going to feel far more comfortable and have much more benefit then the productivity consultant.

The problem with this symptom is that it's hard to sleep well at night because you have that nagging thought in the back of your mind that each meeting with the client is going to be a struggle. So you end up stressed.

The difference between working with a client that is a fit, and working with a client that's not quite a fit, comes down to your ability to deliver value succinctly, easily/naturally, and effectively. And that's stress-free.

Get your Lead Generation happening systematically and effectively and this problem disappears forever.

SYMPTOM #7 IS KEEPING CLIENTS THAT ARE LESS THAN IDEAL. This problem naturally follows on from the previous problem but with a slight variation. Clearly, if we take clients on that are not a fit, then the problem morphs into keeping clients that are not a fit. The variation however, is that sometimes a client starts as a fit but fails to implement on a consistent basis. In that case, you need to be able to gently inform them that they are wasting their money and that you'd be delighted to talk to them again when they have the time/mental space to commit one hundred percent to the implementation of agreed actions.

Once again, establishing effective Lead Generation systems is the key to you being able to relax in choosing both the clients you want to take on board and those clients you wish to retain.

And you're about to find out exactly how to do that.

The Payoff for Solving Your Revenue Problem by Being In Demand

Identifying the benefits or payoff for being In Demand is pretty much a matter of simply reversing the above symptoms. You get to relax, experience the sheer joy of having a greater breadth and depth of choices in every area of your life, feel confident in your abilities and satisfied knowing that you're playing the business game at the highest possible level of your potential.

Do those sort of benefits sound attractive, or did you have a different plan in mind? ☺

PART TWO

MAJOR MISTAKES

ATTEMPTING TO CREATE DEMAND

MOST ADVISORS MAKE THESE MISTAKES

INTRODUCTION

AS MORBID AS it may seem to start with mistakes that Advisors make in attempting Lead Generation, there's actually quite a lot of wisdom in doing so.

This morning I spoke with the previous owner of a business in which I've invested.

The 30-minute meeting I had with him was invaluable, because he outlined what had worked and what had not worked in 10 years of marketing the particular service that the business offers.

I could then confidently and immediately eliminate several options I had previously been considering. In discovering his mistakes, I'd saved myself and the other partners in the business countless dollars and hours and effort.

Additionally, I've seen wasted weeks, months and even years

when Advisors follow Lead Generation advice that is simply never going to work. For example, some play around with Social Media every day for weeks, months and years on end and wonder why they aren't generating any new leads. More on that later.

In addition to the waste of time, energy and money, there is also an increase in negative emotions such as frustration, and as mentioned previously, a lowering of self-esteem that is extraordinarily damaging to the effectiveness of any Advisor.

I actually get a little angry when I hear marketing charlatans, or indeed well-intentioned but inexperienced business coaches, suggesting strategies and tactics that sound good but that will never produce high-quality leads.

In summary, a wise person does *not* learn from his or her own mistakes; they learn from the mistakes of those who have gone before them. Therefore, the chapters contained in this part are likely to be amongst the most valuable in the entire book. I would urge you to study them thoroughly prior to proceeding to Part Three.

MISTAKE #1: PUTTING TACTICS BEFORE STRATEGY

An effective strategy articulates exactly what you need to do in order to create Competitive Advantage, generate enquiries from Ideal Clients, and then scale your Value Delivery. More on that in Part Three.

Tactics, on the other hand, are all about how you will execute that strategy and, of course, in the context of marketing, it includes marketing activity.

Putting Tactics before Strategy is like putting the cart before the horse; in terms of Lead Generation, you simply can't move your business forward.

There are a bunch of Strategic Questions that have to be answered before marketing activity/tactics get underway. Questions such as:

- What does my Ideal Client look like?

- What significant act of transformation can I perform that would be highly desirable for my Ideal Client?

- What Marketing Message does my Ideal Client need to hear or read in order to make an enquiry?

- Where does my Ideal Client hang out and what Mediums will be most effective in reaching out to them with my message?

When these and other critically important Strategic Questions have been answered effectively, then and only then should marketing activity/tactics commence. We'll explore more of the strategic questions in Part Three.

Let's look at an example. Jill is a highly talented Consultant and Trainer. Her specialty is increasing workplace engagement. Her Ideal Client is the CEO of a mid-size company with perhaps 200 to 500 employees. Jill suffers from the Classic Rollercoaster Revenue Syndrome that most Consultants suffer from when they fall prey to the mistake of relying only on Word of Mouth Marketing.

At the bottom of one such rollercoaster ride, she wakes up in the middle of the night in a cold sweat because work is starting to dry up and the normal referrals simply are not coming through. She gets out of bed, makes herself a cup of tea, and goes to a home office where she browses through various online Human Resource e-zines, then buys some advertising space in three of them to promote her business name, contact details, qualifications and the services she provides.

This is what we, in the marketing industry, referred to as "name, rank and serial number" advertising, and unfortunately it just flat out does not work.

The reason why Susan's attempt to generate leads failed is because she hadn't, first of all, answered the critically important strategic questions that need to be effectively answered prior to marketing activity.

Instead of name, rank and serial number advertising, I would recommend that someone like Susan first of all must figure out a Marketing Message that is most likely to generate an enquiry/response.

And in alignment with the questions that appear above, she would then figure out the best Mediums to get that message out to her Market.

For example, an effective Marketing Message for Susan could be *"we show CEOs how to increase engagement and productivity by 25% in just 12 weeks"*.

Think about this: if you were the CEO of a mid-sized organisation and you were concerned about the lack of employee productivity, would you want to know more once you heard that Marketing Message? I would bet you dollars to doughnuts that you would make the enquiry.

In Part Three, Chapter Three, I'll share more on how to create an effective Marketing Message, and in Chapter Four of the same part, I'll reveal the best Marketing Mediums for Advisors.

SOLUTION: answer the tough Strategic Questions prior to undertaking marketing activity.

MISTAKE #2: RANDOM ACTS OF MARKETING

Mistake #1 and #2 are really like two wings of the same bird in that they always go together.

By engaging in random acts of marketing that follow no consistently themed Marketing Message and/or that use ineffective Marketing Mediums, we actually create an "anti-marketing program".

In other words, random acts of marketing are counterproductive because, at best, they damage the quality and power of your brand. At worst, they send mixed, inconsistent and confusing messages out to your marketplace. In the eyes of your Ideal Client, you appear to be dancing the dance of the desperate, like so many of your competitors.

SOLUTION: once you have studied Part Three of this book, you will be in a position to both create an effective Marketing Message and identify the most effective Marketing Mediums through which to promote your Message. Then, you will be able to read about the antidote to random acts of marketing in Part Three Chapter 6, where I show you how to create a Marketing Calendar (critical concept!) so that effective marketing activity is being undertaken systematically week-in and week-out, giving you the joy of a full Pipeline of fresh, highly qualified inbound new client enquiries.

MISTAKE #3: RELYING ON WORD-OF-MOUTH MARKETING

Word-of-Mouth Marketing is very different from Referral Marketing. The former is reactive, in that you wait for a client to mention you to a prospect and, more often than not, you then rely on that prospect to contact you, which may or may not happen. Either way, you are not in control of generating the lead.

Referral marketing, on the other hand, leaves you in control. Using one of many proven, effective referral approaches, you can choose when to generate leads and you have a lot of control over the type and quality of lead you generate.

Don't get me wrong: I love Word-Of-Mouth Marketing because there is a great deal of satisfaction that comes when someone involuntarily mentions the quality of my services to another potential client. But to rely on Word-Of-Mouth Marketing solely for generating leads is like sitting on a stool with only one leg; sooner or later you're going to fall off.

Everyone who has a gram of common sense understands that in the investment world it is unwise to put all of your eggs into the one investment basket. Diversification increases security and the prospect of long-term success.

And it's the same in business. The number "one" is the scariest number in business: relying on *one* client for the majority of your revenue, relying on *one* supplier for the majority of your products/services, relying on *one* key team member to create value, and, in the context of marketing, relying on *one* lead source, whether that be Word-Of-Mouth marketing or a specific advertising medium.

❖ ❖ ❖

SOLUTION: develop a minimum of three Lead Generation mediums so that your Marketing Stool stays upright. More on this in Part Three Chapter Four.

MISTAKE #4: COPYING A HIGH FLOW MODEL

There are quite a few brilliant USA-based marketing gurus. They have built multi-million dollar revenues based on what is commonly referred to in the marketing world as a "Product Funnel".

A Product Funnel is also referred to as a Marketing Funnel, and the essential principle is that the top of a funnel it's very wide and represents a lot of prospects entering your business as subscribers. The objective is to move some of those prospects down the funnel to the point where they start purchasing your core service, and to potentially upsell a lesser number again into a premium-priced service of some sort.

In summary, you induce a lot of people to flow into the top of the funnel to receive some sort of value for free, and you slowly tempt them to move down the funnel to where you begin to, initially, charge a smaller amount of money, and then, later on, a larger amount of money. So this model produces a lot more people at the top of the funnel paying nothing, and as you move down the funnel, less and less people paying more and more.

To most Advisors, this model seems to make a lot of sense; certainly it works exceptionally well for some of the big-name American marketers. Many of them will teach a client how to create a "Lead Magnet" and offer that for free in exchange for the email contact details of visitors to their website. For example, you may be encouraged to offer a series of free video training, a Special Report, a Checklist or Mind Map, or something else that visitors to your website can download for free.

Once subscribed, our American marketing friends teach that you can set up a series of automatic emails ("auto-responders") with more valuable information and the occasional offer to buy something small.

Those who have purchased a relatively less expensive item have theoretically identified themselves as better quality prospects to purchase something more expensive.

I have worked with countless clients who have put such a Product Funnel into place only to discover, to their disappointment and regret, that they have no new leads flowing into the business whatsoever.

The idea of Product Funnel is taught by three categories of marketers. There are the genuinely successful marketers referred to above, who generate multiple millions in revenue and for whom the concept of a Product Funnel, complete with "tripwires" et cetera, works wonderfully. I suspect that the majority of these people teach the concept of the Product Funnel with full integrity and with the belief that this is what everyone should do, because it worked so well for them.

The second category of marketer who recommends the development of Product Funnels contains those who have attended the courses and undertaken the programs of the first category mentioned above. Then, without successfully implementing a Product Funnel of their own, they go out and promote and sell the concept to unwary Advisors.

Most marketers in this category are so desperate for revenue that they shortcut the process of validating what they have been taught, and in doing so perpetuate the ineffectiveness of the traditional Product Funnel concept as it applies to Advisors.

The third category of marketer knows full well that the traditional Product Funnel won't work for most Advisors, but continues to make money from teaching the concept because they have no conscience and are prepared to live knowing that they are ripping people off.

Here's why the traditional Product Funnel probably won't work for you.

To make a Product Funnel work effectively in the way that I've described it above (which is exactly the way it is taught by most marketers), you need a High Flow website. By that I mean you have more than 10,000 visitors to a landing page on your website each week. Of the 10,000 visitors, perhaps 1,000 will opt in by entering their contact details on the landing page in exchange for some form of valuable content.

Those who have opted in will then begin to receive a series of emails with further content and the offer of a small purchase, typically less than $100. In a well-constructed funnel, we might expect 100 to make such a purchase.

Of the 100 people who made that small purchase, there may be five who go on to purchase a more expensive product. And this level of purchasing is the primary aim of people who create product funnels.

All of this works exceptionally well if you have the 10,000 visitors coming to your landing page every week. However, if you have only 100 visitors coming to your website each week, then you simply don't have enough visitors to make your product funnel effective in terms of generating a sufficient amount of high-quality new client enquiries.

This means that as an Advisor setting up a Product Funnel you're likely to waste a lot of time, effort and some money, and end up with nothing to show for it.

Even worse, offering too much free content can actually be counterproductive. The reason for this is that many people who may actually be interested in your core service will, instead of making an enquiry, simply download whatever free content you are offering, tell themselves that they will get around to reading/viewing it at some point, and then fail to ever do so. In the meantime, they have forgotten all about you and you've lost what could have been a very high quality client.

My strategy with most of my clients is to take down most, if not all, of their free downloadable content and offer only one item, which a prospect is typically asked to purchase, and drive all traffic to that offer. In this way, we end up with real high-quality prospects, rather than a larger number of "suspects". The item for purchase is often a book written by my client, or some form of initial "Consult" to see if there is a fit between the prospect's needs and the services provided by my client. "Skin in the game" is the best way to increase the quality of leads flowing into your prospect Pipeline.

I appreciate that many people think that more subscribers and followers must be better than fewer subscribers and followers. But in my experience, that is simply untrue. The quality of a prospect is infinitely more important than the quantity.

Furthermore, I'd encourage you to contemplate the following: most people think that the purpose of a client is to get the sale, whereas it's exactly the other way around: the purpose of the sale is to get a client.

The reason is simple: clients, treated well, will buy again and again and again. Transaction-orientated Advisors are like the proverbial treadmill where they simply chase sales and run harder and faster every year without actually moving forward. It's better to focus on the quality of enquiries and let the quantity look after itself.

SOLUTION: create an intention to generate the highest possible quality of clients even though that may sacrifice the quantity of new subscribers and enquiries. If you have a "Low Flow" model, then don't waste your time, energy and money creating an offer that relies on High Flow.

MISTAKE #5: OFFERING A TRADITIONAL SERVICE

Coco Chanel once said *"in order to be indispensable one must be different"*. If your Ideal Clients perceive that the service you offer is traditional, as opposed to transformational, then you'll have a hard time generating enquiries.

Think about it like this: if you're after an "Acme" brand tennis racket, model "XYZ", and you know that you can get that exact tennis racket from any number of outlets including online stores, then what will your final purchasing decision come down to? Probably the price, right? The reason is simple: your perception, which in this case is quite accurate, is that the product you want to purchase is a commodity item with all the features being identical from each potential supplier. Therefore, price is the only differentiator.

The equivalent is the Advisor who offers, for example, Customer Service training, but who articulates their Value Proposition using the same terminology, the same training duration, the same training methodologies, and similar pricing structure as competitors. To a potential client scouring the market for Customer Service training, picking up brochures, visiting websites, or attending trade shows, most of the trainers look the same.

In Part Three Chapter One, "Magic" will share with you the concept of The Value Slider. You'll discover how to radically transform the way you deliver value to the point where clients will experience your service as transformational rather than traditional. And in Chapter Three "Message" of the same section, I'll show you how to transform your Marketing Message so that the marketplace's perception of your transformational ability is aligned to the reality of what you deliver and how you deliver it.

To be clear, it is *very* likely that you not only need to re-engineer how you deliver value (but not necessarily *what* you deliver) in order to cause a greater number of clients to want to invest in your services, but you'll also need to change your Marketing Message (Part Three, Chapter Three) so that the marketplace's perception of what you do is aligned to the reality of what you do. Think of this as a book and a Book Cover. How do we judge a book? By its cover. Should we judge a book by its cover? Probably not. But nevertheless, we do. So think of the book as a metaphor for what you do, for the value you deliver to a client. And think of the Book Cover as your Marketing Message. We'll dig a lot deeper into these concepts in the next section of this book.

SOLUTION: ensure that the services you offer can transform the personal and/or professional lives of your clients to the point where they say "wow!"

MISTAKE #6: A FAILURE TO NICHE

There's an old saying in the marketing world that the *"riches are in the niches"* and it's very true.

A niche is a small part of the marketplace where you wisely choose to focus your efforts. You have three options when selecting a niche:

1. You can focus on a specific industry or market segment.

2. You can focus on offering a specific service.

3. You can focus on working in a specific geographical location or region.

And naturally you can select either one, two or three of the above.

For example, Jack is a business coach who has failed to target a specific niche and is out there in the marketplace offering some form of twelve-month engagement which will cover business planning, human resource issues, supply and inventory strategies, marketing ideas and plans, quality control systems, and pretty much the whole kit and caboodle; the A to Z of business building.

If a business owner has the money, regardless of the industry they operate in, then Jack will be happy to sign them up. Jack will take on manufacturers, retailers, realtors, multilevel marketers, start-ups, mature businesses, solopreneurs, entrepreneurs, car sales yards, online stores, importers, exporters, and pretty much anyone who can make payments.

What's the problem with that, I hear you ask? Simple: no one has the experience and skill set to effectively support such a wide range of business types right across the board.

That means Jack will receive zero referrals because his engagement with most clients will cease somewhere between the three- and six-month mark as they wake up to the reality that Jack is a generalist who was failing to deliver specialist advice for their particular business.

What makes things doubly difficult for Jack is that he has a much-diminished capability to address specific industry or sector needs when he undertakes his marketing. His messages are generic and many will find it difficult to resonate with his articles, podcasts, special reports, and whatever other content he releases into the marketplace in an attempt to generate leads.

At the risk of appearing self-promotional (which I sincerely hope I am, but in a covert manner ☺) let's contrast Jack's market to my niches.

I target two forms of niches, one being a market niche and the other being a service niche.

The market niche is that I only work with coaches, consultants, Advisors, trainers and teachers, plus others who offer a service. That means I don't work with manufacturers, retailers, realtors, multilevel marketers nor anyone else selling a physical product.

And in respect to my service niche, my "front end" service is all about leading Advisors through a simple, powerfully effective, step-by-step system for creating a continual flow of fresh, high-quality leads into their enquiry Pipeline which is called Leadsology®. I

don't offer to show them how to manage staff, how to improve customer service, how to increase productivity, how to create systems
(other than Lead Generation systems) nor do I offer any number of
other services, even though after 35 years of marketing and management experience I am well qualified to do so.

I'm not saying this to impress you, but rather to impress upon you
the wisdom and effectiveness of picking a niche industry/segment
and/or a niche service. In doing so, you will dramatically improve
the degree of desirability you create among Ideal Clients, and you'll
thereby generate more leads of better quality. Furthermore, your capacity to focus laser-like on the specific needs of the industry/seg-
ment that you've chosen will mean you are far more likely to be able
to deliver value at the sort of transformational level that I've previously referred to. And that will significantly increase your Ideal Clients' motivation level for referring you to their contemporaries.

SOLUTION: choose a niche. Here's how. Make a list of 10 previous
clients who you enjoyed working with and with whom you enjoyed large profits. See if there is a common industry/segment
across 3 to 5 people on that list. If so, you now have a big clue as to
which industry/segment to focus your marketing efforts on. Next,
break all of the work you can do down into a series of segments.
See if you can get to a list of 10 segments. In other words, 10 parts
or aspects of the sort of work you can do. Then pick the top three
that you enjoy performing the most and this will give you a big
clue as to the type of work you should be offering to your chosen
industry/segment.

MISTAKE #7: A FAILURE TO RESPECT PIPELINE PRINCIPLES

A Pipeline means different things to different marketers. For
me, the Pipeline is a metaphor for a place where subscribers and

followers go into, and where some of them are converted into leads that are then in turn converted into clients.

Someone with an empty Pipeline is someone without any prospects or leads. A healthy Pipeline helps you to relax and sleep well every night knowing that you have a constant flow of prospects and enquiries flowing into your business.

If you do verbally communicate your Value Proposition through such efforts as publishing an effective marketing article that is published, or you have new subscribers to your podcast or blog, or new followers on Facebook, or new connections on LinkedIn, or new registrants for a webinar, or new purchasers of your book and so on, then you are filling your Pipeline with prospects who may in turn be converted into lead enquiries who may in turn be converted into clients.

But a Pipeline only works if you respect the principles that make it work. And there are three common violations of those principles that almost every Advisor commits.

Violation number one is that the advisor puts leads into one end of the Pipeline but they don't immediately come out the other end of the Pipeline as clients. So they stop putting the leads into the first end of the Pipeline.

Here's the thing: leads don't always immediately convert to clients. Depending on the industry you work in and the service you provide, it could take weeks or even months for even a high-quality lead to convert into a client. Therefore, if you put a few leads in your Pipeline and the gestation period is say three months but you stop putting leads in after one month, one of the few leads that you put in may actually emerge as a client, but that happy event will then be followed by at least two more months of new-client drought.

Violation number two is exactly the same as violation number one only for a different reason. Violation number two occurs when the Advisor diligently puts leads in the front end of the Pipeline and they start coming out, after a period of time, at the other end of the Pipeline as clients. Then the delighted Advisor stops putting new leads into the front end of the Pipeline because he/she has plenty of work — right now. As I'm sure you've already guessed, once that work is completed the Advisor is then left with an empty Pipeline.

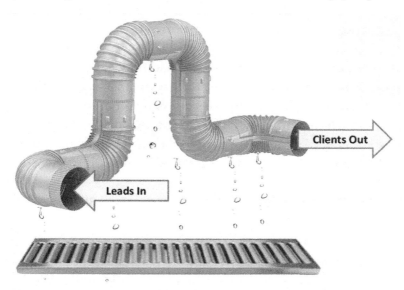

The moral of the story in regard to both violations is that you must continually — ideally every week of the year — be replenishing the front end of your Pipeline with new leads.

The Three B's of Marketing

Which brings us nicely to violation number three. Violation number three is failing to realise that every Pipeline has holes in it where leads will drip out, metaphorically speaking.

What this means is that some people, despite an initial interest in your service, will allow your brand to drop off the radar scope of their mind. You will lose what marketers call "share of mind". This means that the prospect who was initially interested in your service will fail to think of you when they develop a *need* for what you offer. What we need is a drip tray that can catch these prospects and recirculate them back into the Pipeline. And that's where things like webinars and quality Social Media posting come in. These platforms keep your "Brand in their Brain until they are ready to Buy", hence the Three B's of Marketing. That's the purpose of recirculating via the drip tray.

SOLUTION: create a direct response marketing event every single week of the year whereby prospects are given a call to action, be it to book an initial Consult discussion with you or to purchase your book (which also includes the offer of a Consult). This creates a constant flow of new leads going into your Pipeline and therefore, at a later point in time, a constant flow of new clients to work with.

MISTAKE #8: LACK OF LEAD GENERATION SCALABILITY

The term scalability comes from the computer industry. It refers to the capacity of a server to support workstations. For example, if a server is powerful enough to support 100 workstations it is clearly much more "scalable" than a server that can support only 10 workstations. Effectively, what we're talking about in respect to scalable Lead Generation is your capability to generate more leads in less time.

I'm a big fan of Dr Ivan Misner, who is now officially the founder of the world's largest franchise group — Business Network

International, or BNI as it is more commonly known. Ivan is a master of generating leads via networking and certainly when it is done right it can be very effective. But like some other people, I don't enjoy attending networking meetings however I understand that many Advisors find networking groups to be an effective and enjoyable way to prospect for business.

I personally have a couple of other challenges with networking, but before I share them with you I want to reinforce the idea that if you find networking in groups such as BNI (Business Network International) to be effective then you should by all means continue to generate leads from the medium.

That said, let's look at my personal reasons for not attending professional network meetings.

Firstly, attending networking groups means I have to get out of my office here at home next to the beach. I have to drive somewhere, probably a fair distance because I'm not near a major population centre, then I may have to endure traffic hassles and I will most certainly have to find a car park and then I'll have to go and smile weakly with my naturally introverted facial expression and press the flesh with people whom I've never met before and with whom I have no idea whether or not they wash the hands after going to the loo. I'm aware that this might all sound a bit weird to you however I am a little weird and to me this is definitely not something I would look forward to.

Secondly, I love the concept of scalability and that's why I will speak to groups of people, present webinars to groups of people, and sell my book to groups of people. Did you spot the common word denominator? Groups!

Sure, it means I've had to develop new skills and, indeed, I encourage my clients to do the same and I enjoy showing them how. While these new skills represent hurdles that must be overcome, every time one of my clients develops the skill, for example, of generating leads from webinars, or the skill of generating leads through a seminar/workshop, or generating leads through the marketing of their book, then they have just left behind a whole host of competitors who refuse to move their life through those same hurdles.

It's the business world's equivalent of Darwin's theory of natural selection. Adapt or die. Develop or wither. To paraphrase Stewart Brand *"once a new marketing opportunity appears it's like a steamroller and you get to choose whether you're on-board the steamroller or you're part of the road"*.

Solution: find someone, me or someone else, pay them some money, and get them to show you how to develop scalable Lead Generation so that you can generate more fresh, high-quality leads in less time and with less money and with less effort.

Mistake #9: Failure to Establish Know, Like, and Trust

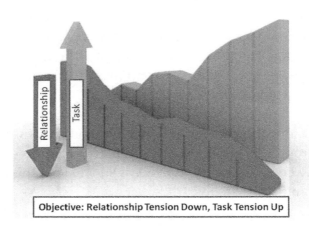

Objective: Relationship Tension Down, Task Tension Up

I first saw my wife across the other side of a crowded room. Corny but true. For me, it was literally love at first sight. I was gone, smitten, game over.

I managed to find a way to introduce myself and we had a coffee, then later we met for lunch and then a bush walk and then … and then … and then … I proposed.

I'm not saying that my Value Proposition was weak, but it took her 869 days to say "yes". But she did say "yes". (I call it "Dripping Tap" marketing!)

But imagine what would have happened if immediately after first seeing her I'd gone up to her and said *"Hi there, I'm Tom; can we get married? Unless you prefer to go to bed first?"*

As attractive as either of those two Value Propositions may have been to me at the time of meeting, I was the "seller" and my future wife needed to get to know me before being presented with such a major "purchasing decision".

I have little doubt that you'd consider me nuts if I'd proposed to her the first time I spoke with her. That being the case, ask yourself how many times you hope that a prospect will buy the first time they come into contact with you or your brand?" Most people would answer *"Pretty much always!"*

The key is to get what I call "relationship tension" down by establishing rapport (*"I know you, like you, and trust you"*) and respect (*"I believe you can help me"*) prior to increasing "task tension," which is what you create when you introduce a Value Proposition that asks the prospect to make a buying decision.

It's very difficult ... make that "extremely difficult", to have a prospect buy anything without first having some positive experience with your brand.

Get relationship tension down before you crank task tension up. Avoid joining the ranks of millions of Advisors who suffer from "Premature Solicitation" syndrome.

To illustrate this concept further, don't expect anyone to make an enquiry, and certainly don't to buy anything, simply because they visited your website, or they liked the look of your LinkedIn profile, or they fancied one of your tweets. And don't expect anyone to make an enquiry or order anything simply because you've sent an email to them unsolicited with what you think is a really cool offer. It is extremely rare to generate any leads, let alone high-quality ones, before you first establish a relationship of know, like, trust, and respect. Like my beautiful wife needed to get to know me before marrying, people need to get to know you, to like you, to trust you, and to respect you prior to making an enquiry or buying any of your services.

SOLUTION: create added-value marketing events/campaigns that add significant value to prospective clients and that impress the socks off them in regard to your expertise and ability to help solve *their* problems and to maximize *their* opportunities.

MISTAKE #10: THE ONE-STEP DISCONNECT

The One Step Disconnect refers to a lack of alignment between your Marketing Message and your Value Proposition. It's a killer of new business. Allow me to illustrate.

A respected colleague of mine, we'll call her Pam, presented a webinar to my network. I can't recall the exact title of the webinar, which had something to do with time management efficiencies and strategies. Pam absolutely knocked it out of the ballpark with her presentation. People loved it. At the end of the presentation, we signalled to attendees that they should stay on the webinar until after the Q&A session if they wanted to know how Pam worked with clients. From memory, well in excess of 90 percent stayed around to hear the details of Pam's program.

What happened next was a shock, albeit of minor proportions. Having got everyone super juiced about the benefits of more-effective time management, Pam then presented details of a broader program on office efficiencies. Now, you and I both know that there is a crossover of common benefits between the subject of time management and office efficiency. For example, if your office is better organised, then you can be wasting less time trying to find things, your follow-up with clients or prospects or suppliers will be more effective and efficient, and so on.

The problem was this: Pam got everyone all hot and sweaty about the super-rich benefits of time management, but the value proposition was couched in different terminology — "office efficiency".

Pam did not get one buyer. Based on my experience, if she had offered a program on time management she would have had at least 10 new clients.

That One Step Disconnect between Pam's Marketing Message as contained in the webinar presentation about the benefits of time management, and the Value Proposition that was articulated as office efficiencies was unfortunately enough to lose her entire audience. Ouch! Pam left a lot of money on the table that day.

Another example.

A client of mine, who we'll call Steve, is one of the smartest guys I know. Steve has developed proprietary methodology for generating greater revenues in large corporate organisations by having the Sales and Marketing divisions collaborate with each other as opposed to what normally happens which is that they fight each other. Steve is tall, good-looking, articulate, and oozes a competent persona and natural charm. All of which will become relevant when I tell you a story.

Early in our engagement of working together, we sharpened up Steve's Marketing Message and created a strategy to run live breakfast events and use his book and other mediums to drive CEOs to the event. If you ever tried to get CEOs to an event, then you'll know that this is not an easy thing to do.

But Steve did a great job with the marketing and ran a few of these events full of CEOs, but the response from the events was dismal. For a while I was stumped. I've run literally hundreds of such events and I'd estimate that more than 90 percent of those events produced a significant quantity of high-quality leads.

So I quizzed Steve about the quality of attendees and that checked out. And so I quizzed him about the venues and that checked out too. And I quizzed about whether or not he remembered to use a feedback form like I had taught him and that checked out too. He seemed to be doing everything that I had taught.

Then, on a hunch, I asked them to send me a copy of the invitation that he was sending to the CEOs that was enticing them to attend the breakfast events. What I discovered is the dreaded One Step Disconnect had crept its way into his process.

While I can't remember the exact details, but it was something like this: Steve would get his most excellent book in front of the CEOs along with a written invitation to attend a breakfast event. However, the invitation's Value Proposition offered the opportunity to network with other CEOs and discuss challenges and opportunities with other like-minded, growth-orientated CEOs so that they could share their solutions and experiences.

Can you spot the One Step Disconnect? Steve's Marketing Message contained in the invitation to attend the breakfast event was based around networking with other CEOs.

However, when he presented his Value Proposition at the end of the breakfast, it was all about creating collaboration between each CEO's Sales and Marketing divisions. That's a big disconnect between the Marketing Message and the Value Proposition.

SOLUTION: ensure that whatever Marketing Message you create (more on that In Part Three Chapter Three) is completely and 100 percent aligned with your Value Proposition (the description of your service including its features and benefits) so that there are zero surprises for your prospects.

MISTAKE #11: NO BAIT TRAIL

I first developed the Bait Trail Principle back in 2008 when I noticed too many Advisors were confusing high-quality prospects by providing them with too much information all at once.

I erroneously based my theory of the Bait Trail on the story of Hansel and Gretel whom I thought had followed a trail of lollies laid out along a forest track leading to the rather improbable house made of lollies and owned by a wicked witch with a very large cauldron.

(How on earth the Brothers Grimm thought that boiling children alive in a cauldron was a suitable fairy tale for young kiddies is beyond me).

As it turns out, there was no such trail of lollies on the path but rather simply two little kids getting lost in a forest and stumbling upon a child's culinary delight in the form of several tons of sugar and chocolate moulded into the shape of walls and roof.

So I was wrong about Hansel and Gretel, but I was right about the Bait Trail Principle.

Here's how it works. We vastly over estimate the amount of information that otherwise incredible brains can process at any one given point in time.

What the Bait Trail Principle recognises is that people are far more likely to take action if they are presented with one clear call to action and an absolute minimum of information communicated around their options other than a clear articulation of the benefits that will result from taking action.

Allow me to illustrate with an example. For many years now I have regularly interviewed people I regard as having something special to offer to my network. This keeps my network of subscribers and followers well nurtured with high-quality fresh content, which means they are more likely to stay followers and to stay subscribed.

When I first started approaching people to interview them, I didn't know about the Bait Trail Principle. I'd invite them to be interviewed and then tell them about how we would publish it, then tell them about the possible joint-venture opportunity if everything went well and tell them about how we could cross-market to each other's networks and so on. In short, my approach was so comprehensive that the size of the Value Proposition resembled the phone book of a small African nation.

The result was that we failed to generate a response from the vast majority of the people we approached. This was around about the time I started to learn about copywriting.

So I took a fresh look at the copy that I was writing and using in my approach for potential interviewees. Fortunately, I saw my mistake. I was showing my prospects every step along the path toward the witch's house.

I then changed my approach to showing my prospective interviewees only the next step that I wanted them to say yes to, similar to laying out a series of sweets on a path to tempt people to take another step and yet another step and yet another step until they have arrived at the place that you want them to be.

By way of another example, imagine for a moment that you are a senior executive in a multinational and you are speaking to a corporate Trainer because you are interested in their services. The Trainer explains how she works with clients: she conducts an initial consult which runs for 60 minutes where she will diagnose your business needs and see if you have a fit between your needs and her service. She then goes on to explain that, if you have a fit, there is an initial six-week period of analysis at the end of which she would present a report. This is followed by a 12-week training program and then the opportunity to filter down the protein program from the senior managers into each division, and then the opportunity to go from one state to another and from one country to another. And, finally, she also can provide consulting services and so on and so forth. She continues to itemise pricing at each stage.

Now just take a quick look at the size of the above paragraph and you'll see why even smart executives get frozen like a deer in the headlights when presented with such a complex Value Proposition.

Using the Bait Trail Principle, all that the corporate Trainer would communicate to the executive is that she has 60 minutes available to sit down with you and that will reveal how much productivity upside your organisation has, and what you should do to take advantage of that potential.

Using the Bait Trail Principle, there would be no mention of six-week diagnostic analysis exercises or anything else that may (or may not) happen after the initial consult. All you need to hear as the executive is the next step and some compelling reasons to take that step (identifying productivity upside and what needs to be done to make it happen) and then you are exponentially more likely to take action.

SOLUTION: I am frequently asked about how long a webpage should be or how long a sales letter should be and so forth and so on. My answer is this *"as long as it needs to be in order to get the job done and then as short as possible"*. The "job" is generally to elicit an enquiry.

That being the case, when you phone a prospect, or when you email a prospect, or when you close out a webinar, or when you do anything where you want to move a prospect closer to a purchasing decision, only give them the next step and a good reason to take it.

MISTAKE #12: THINKING THAT CHEAPER PRICES WILL INCREASE DEMAND

The person in the marketplace who is most sensitive about your prices is you. I found this to be true time and time again: the person selling a service is the person most concerned about the perception of its expense.

Today I met with a client and suggested that he undertake some mystery shopping with his competitors. In other words, I suggested that he call his competitors and make enquiries, not lying at all about who he was or where he was from but simply asking for information packs to be sent out and about pricing and about other features of his competitors' services. I clearly instructed him that, if he was asked who he was, then he should respond honestly and openly and offer a full exchange of information.

He told me that the first phone call he made to a business he perceived to be his most direct competitor revealed something of a chink in that competitor's armour.

He got hold of someone and asked about the features of their service and about pricing. The person at the other end of the phone stated the price and then added *"the reason we are so expensive is …"* and then proceeded to defend the pricing which, in my view at least, was not expensive at all, and in fact was some 50 percent cheaper than my client's pricing for a comparable service. Like I said, the people who are selling service are the ones who are most sensitive about its price.

I have lost count of the number of clients I have convinced to increase their prices significantly despite the obstacle presented by their fears around failing to bring new clients on board. Of all the clients who proceed with club price increases, of which there must surely be dozens, every single one said they wished they had done this years ago and rued the fact that they had been leaving so much money on the table, so to speak.

My clients tend to offer premium-style services. Top of the shelf stuff. No compromises, only the most effective and best quality services. If you are similar, then here is your wake-up call: a failure to charge premium prices for a premium service will repel prospects, not attract them.

Furthermore, premium-priced services attract better-quality clients who are more motivated to implement your advice, who will therefore gain immensely more value than other people, and who will consequently refer more people back to you.

This, even apart from the fact that you will make more money and have more cash in your bank account as a result of even one client engagement, is an extraordinarily powerful reason to ensure that you are one of the most expensive suppliers in the marketplace.

Premium-quality clients just flat out do not respect cheap.

Lastly, on the subject of premium pricing, having premium priced your main service, you should then additionally create what you perceive to be a super expensive, super-duper offering.

I was in discussion with another client of mine, Mark, who is a brilliant corporate trainer and I suggested that he create a more fully featured program and charge twice his usual fee of $25,000. So that's a $50,000 program. He asked me why I thought he should do that. I replied with a question: *"Mark, how many $50,000 programs will you sell if you don't have the $50,000 program?"*.

Now, Mark is a highly intelligent person, so it only took another second to respond with the obvious answer that he would sell absolutely zero $50,000 programs if he did not have a $50,000 program on offer.

"But who would buy it?", Mark asked.

I said to Mark that I would guarantee that at least once a year or at the very least once every two years he would sit in front of a CEO who simply had to have the most expensive program on offer. If it's in the budget, then he/she will always want the best.

Personally, I would prefer to buy half as often and spend twice as much and hopefully get three times the quality.

Apple recently launched a new range of the iWatch. The range consisted of three options. There was $399 iWatch. There was a $599 iWatch. And there was a $14,000 iWatch. Why would Apple produce such an expensive iWatch? The reason is simple: as previously stated, some people just have to have the most expensive product on offer. Go figure.

SOLUTION: if you offer a premium product, then match it with premium pricing. Cheap will do exactly the opposite of attracting new clients and it will also most certainly repel premium-quality clients. Additionally, create a service that is twice the price or whatever your poor service currently is.

Mistake #13: The Marketing Message Doesn't Get Cut Through

Because creating Marketing Messages that generate high-quality leads is my specialty, I'm going to delve into this in considerable detail in Part Three Chapter Three. Therefore, I'll not spend too much time on it right here.

I've mentioned "name, rank and serial number" Marketing Messages before, but just to reiterate: we need to have a Marketing Message articulated in such a way that, when an Ideal Client reads it or hears it, they are compelled to ask for more information.

To illustrate this point simply and quickly, just to whet your appetite for later, imagine that you are committed to grow your business (which given that you have bought this book you probably are) and that I was a business coach (which I'm not) and that you and I were talking at a dinner party and that you asked me what I did for a living. And let's say I responded with *"I'm a business coach"*.

At this point there is a high likelihood that you will mumble something like "that's nice" and slowly walk away.

Whereas if my response was *"I show Advisors how to generate one new, premium-quality client every single week — oh, and I guarantee that"*. At this point, there is also a very high likelihood of something — but this time it's the likelihood that you would ask me how I did that. That is a living example of how an effective Marketing Message gets cut through and elicits an enquiry. More on that in Part Three Chapter Three.

SOLUTION: create a Marketing Message that compels your Ideal Clients to request more information.

MISTAKE #14: THINKING IT'S ABOUT A BETTER MOUSETRAP

I covered this briefly in Part One under the section entitled "Your Revenue Problem And The Solution," but such an important concept is worth expanding on.

Someone once said that if you build a better mousetrap the world will beat path to your door. But as Harvey McKay responded *"the hell it will, it's the marketing that makes the difference"*. Never a truer sentence was spoken.

As I mentioned previously, if your clients think that your service is better than good, then it's better than good and you should quit messing with it and simply rinse and repeat what you're doing. But most human beings get bored relatively easily. That means that, even when we have a thing that works incredibly well, we want to mess with it. There is some truth in the old adage "if it ain't broke, don't fix it" but of course we also need to recognise the need for continual innovation. But not continuous changes. There's a big difference.

When you create an effective Marketing Message and when you get that effective Marketing Message out through effective Marketing Mediums (more on this in Part Three Chapter Four) and thereby get in front of Ideal Clients, you *will* generate enquiries.

And because you've done such a good job of creating a highly desirable Value Proposition, when a prospective new client enquires as to how you work with your clients <u>they don't really care too much about the answer.</u>

To illustrate the point, if I have a toothache and I go to the dentist because I'm in pain and the dentist looks at my tooth and tells me that he/she needs to inject into my gum and extract the tooth and will take an hour, then I'll tell him or her okay let's do it.

However, if I have a toothache and I go to the dentist because I'm in pain and the dentist looks at my tooth and tells me to take a tablet and that the pain will go away, then I'll tell him or her okay let's do it.

And if I have a toothache and I go the dentist because I am in pain and the dentist looks at my tooth and tells me that if I stand on my head and wiggle the little pinky on my left foot three times in a counter clockwise direction then, if I'm in enough pain and if I trust my dentist, then I'm sure as hell going to try it at least once.

What's my point? My point is this: to a large extent, people don't care how you do what you do so long as they get the benefit that was embedded in your Marketing Message that attracted them to find out more in the first place.

Too many trainers, consultants, coaches, teachers and other Advisors try to impress their clients by dazzling them with complexity and telling how much time they'll be spending with the client. Big mistake. The vast majority of clients want you to keep things as simple as possible, for you to take up as little of their time as possible, and to deliver the results as fast as possible — and in the easiest consumable form possible. More on this in Part Three Chapter One under The Value Slider.

Solution: create a transformational service and then quit messing with it and focus instead on marketing and scaling your Value Delivery.

Mistake #15: Confusing Marketing with Selling

As a young man, I cut my teeth on selling one of the toughest products in the world to sell: life insurance.

The reason that the life insurance industry spent so much money on sales training was that they were such lousy marketers (and they still are).

But even though I was pretty darn good at selling, I was always, always, always fascinated by the idea of marketing, so much so that I even applied for a position, any position, in the marketing department of the life insurance company whose products I was selling.

So what's the difference between marketing and selling and why is it so important?

Think of it like this: if bees were a metaphor for clients and you wanted more bees, then you have a couple of options. Firstly, you can go and buy yourself a net, find a garden that's full of flowers and go running through the garden chasing the bees trying to capture them in your net.

That's very stressful for you and, even though the bees have the tiniest of all brains, it can get kinda stressful for them as well, I'm sure.

Or you can go and get yourself a jar of honey and take the lid off of it and set it on your back doorstep and watch as the bees come flying in.

Which is not stressful at all. On the contrary, it is relatively simple and relatively easy and completely stress free. Even the bees like the idea.

Here is the reality of sales: people love to buy and they hate to be sold. That being the case, any overt form of selling is a form of an anti-marketing, in that it will actually repel premium-quality prospects. Almost without exception, my clients are marketing to intelligent and sophisticated buyers who can smell a sales technique from a mile off. So quit selling and start marketing.

Solution: create the equivalent of the metaphorical honey pot to attract premium-quality enquiries. Find someone who can show you how to create honey pots in the form of webinars, seminars, books and other lead generators which are extraordinarily effective when done well.

Mistake #16: Thinking Social Media Will Generate Leads

There's a whole lot of hooey going around the marketing world about Social Media. Perhaps you've even tried to increase your subscribers or attract new leads by Blogging or Podcasting or Article Marketing or Facebooking or Tweeting or Instagraming or using whatever mixture within the Social Media universe of options touted by mistaken but well-meaning people.

Is it possible to generate high-quality leads from Social Media? Yes. But it takes years of almost daily effort. And there are so many other ways to generate high-quality leads almost instantly that for the life of me I cannot understand why anyone would want to *start* the Lead Generation effort with Social Media. This is like wanting an apple but, instead of picking the "low-lying fruit," you end up hiring a hoist and going straight to the top of the tree to pick your apple.

Social Media is a great Drip Tray (see Mistake #7 above) and is ideal for "keeping the Brand in the Brain until they are ready to Buy". But in the short term, it's completely lousy at generating high-quality lead enquiries from people who are ready to buy.

I'm amazed at the vanity of some people who think if they write a blog about what they had for breakfast that people would actually be interested in reading it. And even when we go to a higher level of content-style marketing, it is still extraordinarily difficult to create content that is of sufficient quality to capture a prospect's attention, keep them engaged, and then generate an enquiry.

I'm an avid supporter of Social Media as a Marketing Medium to keep the brand in the brain until ready to buy. But don't start with it. Instead, start with direct response, call-to-action style marketing where you can actually generate real leads of high quality.

Solution: develop a direct response, call-to-action marketing event of some description every week of the year. Once you have that well-established, then and only then develop Social Media marketing to keep the brand in the brain until ready to buy.

PART THREE
THE MODEL

THE 10-STEP IN DEMAND
LEAD GENERATION MODEL

INTRODUCTION

LEADSOLOGY® IS LIKE any other highly advanced skill set in that there are a lot of sub-skills, or component parts, that, when mastered, lead to a professional performance and highly desirable result.

For example, if you look at a Serena Williams or a Roger Federer playing tennis, there are literally more than 100 subtle nuances about their stance, grip changes, place on the court, backswing, follow-through, posture, timing in hitting the ball, where they hit the ball to, the amount of topspin, and much more. Each of these subtle sub-skills has been honed from the moment they could first toddle around and hold a little mini-tennis racket. When we watch such sports stars perform, they often make it look sublimely easy when, in fact, it's certainly anything but for a beginner.

So how does someone become a great tennis player, or a great golfer, or a great musician, or a great artist, or a great orator, or a great Leadsologist?

The answer is the same: you find someone who has figured out the techniques, you pay them some money, and you ask them to Mentor/Coach/Teach/Train you as you develop the skills. Because just like learning a sport or a musical instrument, practice does not make perfect.

Perfect practice makes perfect.

In other words, unless you are practising the *right* techniques (as illustrated in this book), and unless you have a Mentor/Coach/ Teacher/Trainer who can study the technique you are learning and point out improvement opportunities as you execute them, it is fairly likely that you will simply embed poor-quality habits into your practice, and thereby perpetuate poor-quality performances.

Which brings us to the Leadsology® Model.

Leadsology® lays out the 10 component parts that, when embedded into your business, create a systematic, controllable and predictable flow of high-quality, fresh inbound leads coming into your business.

Getting good at Leadsology® is just like getting good at a sport, or getting good at singing or playing an instrument well, or any other skill set in the world. You need to have the right component parts to practice and implement so that you can continually increase the effectiveness of your Leadsology® skill set.

So let's have a look at the 10 Leadsology® component parts that

will have you Being In Demand. Here's an overview of the model
to start with:

a

CHAPTER ONE:
THE MAGIC

MAGIC IS ALL about the transformation you bring into a client's life or business.

And one of the big Strategic Questions that needs to be answered is how you will deliver that Magic to a client in a way that it is both differentiated from that of your competitors and more desirable. They are the two key words when it comes to marketing strategy: Differentiated and Desirable.

In the previous section of this book, I noted that having a traditional service (or being perceived as having a traditional service) is akin to trying to sell the same tennis racket that 100 or more of your competitors also try to sell. An accountant/CPA who presents themselves as a traditional accountant has tens of thousands of competitors. If you include offshore options such as India, Eastern Europe and parts of Asia, then that accountant/CPA has literally hundreds of thousands, if not millions of competitors.

However, if that account/CPA changes their Marketing Message and Value Proposition from talking about "doing the books," tax returns, profit-losses, and balance sheets to something like "we increase the amount of cash in a qualifying client's bank account by $25,000 or more every single month," then that creates some Magic that is both differentiated and highly desirable indeed.

I'm sure that you'll agree that in the above contrasting examples the transformational Marketing Message and Value Proposition eliminate virtually all direct competitors, and therefore provide the basis for extraordinarily effective Lead Generation that results in Being In Demand.

I also mentioned previously that we have to deal with both the "Book" as well as the "Book Cover". In other words, it's not just the perception (Book Cover) that we need to re-engineer, but it's also the actual service/advice/Magic that you deliver. In this chapter, I'm only going to deal with the Magic/Book. When we get to Chapter 3 of this part, then I'll deal with the Message/Book Cover.

There are two main concepts that I'll present in this chapter: the first is The Value Slider and the second The Desirability Rating. The first concept deals with the issue of Differentiation and the second deals with the issue of Desirability.

Once you tick all boxes in both of these concepts, you've got yourself some significantly attractive Magic that you can then begin to Market.

THE VALUE SLIDER

This concept alone has done more to generate demand than any other single concept I've developed or taught over the past 35 years. So listen up!

There are seven characteristics that your Ideal Clients will be looking for in your service. The name of the game is to maximise the level of Desirability for as many of the seven characteristics as you can.

The seven characteristics are as follows:

1. A *measureable* transformation

2. A *significantly better* transformation

3. A transformation that's delivered *faster*

4. A better *return on investment* (NOT cheaper!)

5. The transformation that's *simpler* to implement

6. A transformation that's *easier* to achieve

7. A transformation that's *relevant* to the client's needs

(Keywords above are in italics)

I'm sure you'll agree that if your Value Proposition offers a measurable and significantly better transformation that's delivered faster, simpler and easier and is more relevant to your client's needs and can also demonstrate a significantly better return on investment than your competitors, then you've just got yourself a new client.

When it comes to your existing services, there are no sacred cows. Some of what you currently do you may be able to keep, but some of it you may have to discard. As one famous author said when asked what the secret was to creating a tight plot: *"kill your darlings"*.

Let's have a quick look at these characteristics one by one.

A *measureable* transformation

You'll either be providing a service to a business or to an individual. The former is referred to as B2B, or business to business, and the latter is referred to as B2C, or business to consumer.

If small business owners are your B2B target market, then the primary motivations in respect to the measurable transformation you offer will probably be more clients and more revenue/cash in the bank.

If corporate executives are your B2B target market, then the primary motivations will be more about revenue, profit, market share, customer satisfaction, career advancement, and productivity.

If you're in the B2C (business to consumer) segment, then health/ energy improvements or healthier relationships will be big motivators.

But regardless of which B2B market you are in, or which B2C market you are in, it is fundamentally important that you provide your clients with a measure of transformation. Preferably, this is a transformation that is measurable in metrics i.e. numbers of some description, be that dollars or percentages. If that's not possible, then we revert to subjective measures which may include how a person is feeling on a scale of 1 to 10, or some other feeling-based measure.

A *significantly better* transformation

This one is pretty easy to figure out. Your Value Proposition and Value Delivery can't be about incremental improvements. It can't be about little tiny improvements for the screamingly obvious reason that no one is going to get excited about this idea. The measurable improvement on offer won't be desirable if it's measured in one dollar or one percent; it's got to be measured in terms that are exciting for the Ideal Client relative to the size of their business (B2B) or to the size of their challenge/problem/opportunity (B2C).

For example, no CEO in his/her right mind is going to hire you if you're talking about a 1 percent increase. But if you talk about a 25 percent increase — in practically any result area they are targeting — then they probably will want to know more.

A word of caution: if you are in a sophisticated market, then the articulation of your significantly better transformation needs to not only evoke interest/mild excitement, but also be believable. The same CEO who failed to get excited about a 1 percent increase is also not going to get excited about a 100 percent increase in results because they will find that sort of value proposition unbelievable.

(I'll give you some specific examples that will bring the seven characteristics to life in the last part of this section.)

A transformation that's delivered *faster*

As an example of delivering a transformation faster, imagine that you're in the market to hire a new trainer, or consultant, or coach to increase revenue by 25 percent. You have two highly recommended Advisors to choose from. One guarantees to show you how to achieve that over a 12-month period, and the other guarantees to show you how to achieve that over 12-week period. Which one would you choose?

At this stage, you need to put out of your mind, especially if you are a trainer or a consultant or a coach, how that objective can be achieved in such a short space of time. Never confuse promise with delivery. We need to first of all figure out, not what you can currently do/achieve, but what your Ideal Client needs to hear/read in order to want to know more — that is, to initiate an enquiry.

We then work backwards from that thing they need to hear or read, and figure out how the heck we can deliver it. Of course, it is critically important that we deliver, if not over-deliver, on the promise. However, it is equally important to understand that going into the marketplace with a Value Proposition and Value Delivery that fails to generate enquiries is an exercise in prolonged futility and frustration.

To further illustrate the point, let's go back to my dentist analogy. Imagine that I'm at the dentist with my toothache and she tells me that she can take the pain away for $300. I then ask the dentist how long it will take and the dentist thinks for a moment and says *"about 10 minutes"*. I instinctively react with surprise, saying *"10 minutes?"*. The dentist thinks again for a moment and says *"yes it does sound like quite a lot for only 10 minutes, but I tell you what I can do if you like, I'll make it last an hour. Would you prefer that?"* I then think for a moment and tell her that 10 minutes sounds just fine.

A better *return on investment* (NOT cheaper!)

I've discussed the mistake of thinking that lowering prices will increase demand and I've pointed out proven reasons why in a premium market cheaper prices will actually have the opposite effect and will reduce demand.

So I'm pretty sure we'll both be on the same wavelength when I point out that, provided you are in front of a prospective Ideal Client (they are aware of their need for what you have, *they have the money*, and the timing is perfect), then getting a return on their investment is a gazillion times more important than the price.

Allow me to illustrate.

Once again, imagine you are in the market to hire a coach/mentor.

Let me introduce you to Jack. He is a kindly old soul who is now retired but is prepared to mentor you and pass on the experience he's gleaned over his many years as a bank manager. He is going to charge you $100 for the engagement.

However, things don't go so well. It turns out that Jack likes the odd nip of whiskey starting fairly early in the day. He also is very fond of reminiscing over old times to the point where you're subjected to the same long-winded stories time and again. But Jack's a nice bloke with a good heart and so you persist.

But after three months, you finally summon up the courage to email Jack and say something like: *"hey, it's been great and I really appreciate your help but I need to put our engagement on hold for a little while because I'm kind of tied up with a whole lot of stuff right now"*. Yes, that's right: you write the Dear John letter to Jack — *"I hate to leave, but is not you, it's me"* — you give Jack the oldest break-up line in the book.

You then meet Jill. Jill is a professional business coach with a proven track record, but she charges $3,000 a month. Ouch. But she comes highly recommended and so you start working with her and after three months she has transformed your business. Revenue has increased $30,000 a month and you're working fewer hours than you ever have before. Very cool. A transformation!

Okay, so let's conclude. Out of Jack and Jill, who turned out to be the most expensive?

My answer would be Jack because, even though he only charged $100, you wasted a whole lot of time and energy and achieved exactly nothing.

Jill on the other hand delivered a far superior return on investment. You invested a total of $9,000 and you got to enjoy an additional $30,000 every month in your bank account. That's a return on investment that is probably incalculable, but which would certainly run into the many thousands of percent.

When you can demonstrate a return on investment that's significant, and preferably guaranteed, the world *will* beat a path to your door and you *will* Be in Demand

A transformation that's *simpler* to implement

"If you want to make a lot of money

and build a great big reputation

take something that's actually quite simple

and add a really big complication"

I wrote the above ditty after reviewing a proposal from a consultant who was pitching for business with one of my clients. The

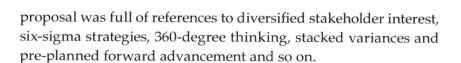

proposal was full of references to diversified stakeholder interest, six-sigma strategies, 360-degree thinking, stacked variances and pre-planned forward advancement and so on.

Seriously? Give me a break.

Now I appreciate this was only the consultant's Book Cover, but it is fair to assume that anyone reading that proposal would at the very least unconsciously conclude that the implementation of the proposal would be equally complex.

I advised my client to look for another consultant, which he did.

Your job as an advisor is not to impress a potential client or indeed an actual client, with the breadth and span of your knowledge. Rather, it is to make everything, as Einstein said, *"as simple as possible, but no simpler"*. That means make a thing as simple as possible but not to the point of degrading the effectiveness of what you're doing.

A transformation that is *easier* to achieve

This follows on from the above point. If you could transform someone's body from fat and unhealthy to slim, toned, beautiful, and energetic with one capsule, then there is no doubt whatsoever that the world would beat a path to your door. Unfortunately, it doesn't work like that.

But the point remains the same: the easier you can make it for a client to receive the Value Delivery then the more In Demand you will become.

A transformation that's *relevant* to the client's needs

A colleague of mine developed special swimming pools for Little People. Just to clarify for those who may not be up with the latest terminology, these wonderful souls were previously referred to most inappropriately as dwarves. Like you, I'm sure, political correctness has gone too far in certain areas, but this is not one of them. Because these people don't hang out with Snow White; they hang out with people like you and me.

Back to the point of my story. The backstory to the above was that Michael was teaching a regular swimming class one day for a child when the mother of a Little Person approached and asked if he would teach her son how to swim. Now naturally, as the son was not yet an adult, he was a very Little Person indeed. So much so that he was unable to stand up in the shallow end of the swimming pool.

Michael so regretted having to turn down this mother's request simply because he didn't have an adequate facility to train Little People, that he decided to modify the training pool to accommodate Little People and their families.

Today, Michael runs a seven-figure swim training business across the country teaching Little People and their families the joy of swimming. That is a perfect example of being In Demand by creating a transformation that carefully targeted, and therefore was 100 percent relevant, to the Ideal Client's needs.

The more specific your solutions target clients' needs, the more In Demand you will become.

THE VALUE SLIDER – AN EXAMPLE

Let's look at how this plays out with a specific client. You'll see in the chart below that our seven characteristics are listed on the right-hand side and their opposites are listed on the left-hand side.

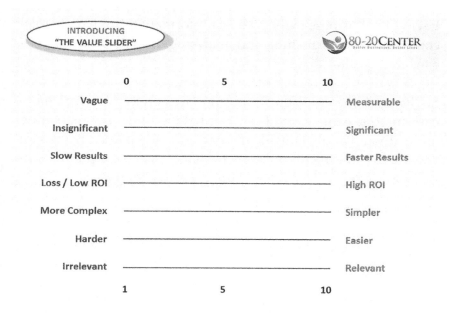

The client's name is Adam. And Adam is the Profits Leak Detective. I won't state all the following details with hundred percent accuracy because I want to protect Adam's intellectual property to some degree. However, the example serves well to illustrate the power of The Value Slider in creating Being In Demand.

Prior to working The Value Slider and his Marketing Message, Adam's Value Proposition was articulated around the idea of plugging the profit leaks in a business owner's operation. The concept was that the owner of the business didn't need to get any more clients on board, and didn't need to work any longer or harder. They simply needed to work with Adam for six months or so and he'd show them how to plug the "profit leaks" by stopping financial wastage, increasing the success rate of client proposals, and so on.

Adam's Value Delivery involved gaining access to the accounts, having the business owner request information from his/her accountant, and a crunching and analysing of some pretty significant and varying streams of data.

So the fundamental Value Proposition was pretty powerful: more cash in your bank account without having to do any marketing and without having to work any longer or any harder. But Adam was finding it difficult to create Demand. When we put his Value Proposition on The Value Slider prior to reengineering, this is what it looked like.

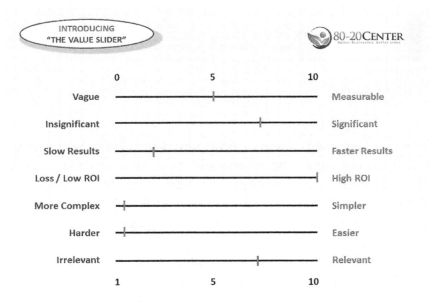

(The Value Slider images are taken from a presentation on the subject, so please excuse the branding.)

Adam rated a 5 on a scale of 10 for being able to deliver a measurable difference, although in this example, which is the "before" scenario, he had not specified the amount of extra revenue a business owner might enjoy in the bank account at the end of every month.

He scored 7/10 for being able to make a significant difference, but only 2/10 for getting results faster because this was a six-month deal.

In respect to a Return On Investment, he scored a 10 out of 10. He charged just $15,000 for the six-month assignment and very often he was able to leave his clients with at least $15,000 shaven off every single month for the rest of their business career.

One of the downfalls of Adam's original Value Proposition was that it was quite a complex operation, so we graded him 1/10 for that. In tandem with the complexity of analysing multiple streams of data, there was the added difficulty of actually obtaining accurate data.

The process involved a number of roadblocks, most notably getting the client's accountant to respond to various information requests. So in respect to making it easier, the score was also only a 1/10.

Adam recorded a 7/10 for being relevant to the client's needs, which in hindsight may be just a tad harsh. I scored 7/10 for that aspect of the Value slider simply because a lot of his Ideal Clients weren't even aware that they might have profit leaks, so they weren't looking for his specific service.

Adam's total score out of a potential 70 was 34. When we convert that into a percentage, his In Demand score was 48 percent.

So having measured his original Value Proposition on the Value slider, we then set to re-engineering.

I suggested to Adam that we apply the 80/20 principle to his work and also figure out the 10 things that made the biggest difference in a short space of time. Instead of asking the business owner to get all the data, we simply hired a virtual assistant offshore and gave them permission to talk to the accountant and access, on a read-only basis, the books and bank accounts.

I suggested that we also do the whole thing in six weeks instead of six months, and that we Message the Magic more sharply by telling the business owner that will guarantee another $10,000 in their bank account by the third month.

Naturally, that meant we had to pre-qualify who to take on as a client, but we have to do that anyway.

We still charge the same $15,000 fee, but we don't insist on all of it up front. Instead, we cash flow the payments over three months and offer a guarantee that if, at the end of the first month, the client wasn't 100 percent confident that the work Adam was doing was more than on track to fulfil our value proposition (another $10,000 in their bank account each month) then they could have their money back.

In doing so, we reduced the feeling of risk in the mind of the Ideal Client. We also created a degree of reverse psychology, because we were telling the marketplace that this minor miracle could only be achieved "for qualifying clients".

As an added bonus for Adam, we were reducing the duration of the engagement for the client, and Adam's time input also dropped dramatically. He's managed to scale Value Delivery by applying the 80/20 principle, and financially and time-wise he's a whole lot better off than before.

Here's what Adam's Value Slider looked like after our little re-engineering work:

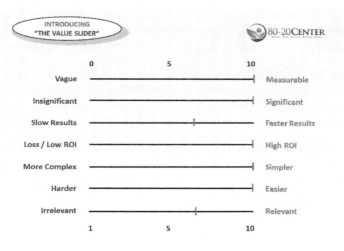

You'll note we've moved to 10/10 for measurability because a Value Proposition now contains a specific dollar figure per month that the client will realize.

Similarly, because we've been much more specific in terms of our Value Proposition, the significance of the benefits is much greater in the mind of the client, so we can score ourselves 10/10 for this part as well.

Faster results is scored 7/10 because it still is not an overnight transformation; it's still a whole lot better than the 2/10 we scored previously.

Post transformation, we kept the Return On Investment score the same at 10/10.

The introduction of our offshore VA together with gaining user-only access to all existing data and account information made the whole process infinitely simpler and easier for both the business owner client as well as Adam. Hence, the maximum score of 10/10 is awarded for both of these characteristics.

And the score for relevance remains at 7/10 for the same reasons I've outlined previously. But let's look at the In Demand score. After our transformation, our score is a total of 64 out of a possible 70 which converts to a 91 percent In Demand score compared to the previous score of 48 percent.

Now naturally, this is a subjective analysis of the differences in marketplace demand and it is therefore not research-proven. However, even Blind Ned sitting in his "common sense corner" could see that, post transformation, the Value Proposition will create more demand than the original Value Proposition.

In conclusion, I recommend that you run the Value slider over your own Value Proposition and see where and how you can increase the score for as many of the seven characteristics as possible. The results truly can be nothing short of transformational, provided you start with what a client would want, rather than with what you've already got. *"Kill your darlings"*.

THE DESIRABILITY RATING

As mentioned before the Desirability Rating is a tool you can use to confirm and/or improve your competitive advantage against competitors.

Step one is to create a list of your Ideal Clients' most important Values/Needs/Motivators. I regard each of those three words as being interchangeable in this context.

By way of example, here is a list of my Ideal Client's Values/Needs/Motivators:

1. Effectiveness: what I deliver *will* produce results.

2. 80/20 Simplicity: clients want minimum effort to produce maximum results.

3. Ease of implementation: clients really like the step-by-step nature of my work.

4. Peace of mind: clients love the fact that I guarantee my work.

5. A significant return on investment.

6. Zero hype — only the stuff that actually works.

7. Collaboration — working *together* so we get a better result synergistically.

8. Rational, logical, zero fluff or BS.

9. A shorter, faster path to the result.

10. A high level of competence that comes from working with a reputable brand.

Step two is to rate how important each Value/Need/Motivator is in the mind of your Ideal Client.

Step three is to rate your ability to meet each of those needs/wants/values on a scale of 1 to 10, one being that you completely suck at it, and 10 being that you are knocking it out of the ballpark.

And in step four, you rate your major competitors, and any indirect but significant competitors, in terms of their ability to meet each of the Needs/Wants/Values.

Here's a screenshot example from one of my clients who is a corporate trainer/coach/consultant specialising in increasing the productivity of teams (I ghosted out the names of the individual essences to preserve anonymity):

Name:	Desirability Rating				Date:
Increase measurable employee productivity and engagement by 25%					
Ideal Clients' Values/Needs/Motivators (List in order of priority)	Client Value Rating (10 = most)				
1 Gets real results	10	10	7	7	10
	Sub Total:	100%	70%	70%	100%
2 Fast - doesn't take too much time to get to answers	9	9	5	4	5
	Sub Total:	100%	56%	44%	56%
3 Step by Step and Easy to implement	10	10	5	5	8
	Sub Total:	100%	50%	50%	80%
4 Easy to get buy in of team/ staff	9	6	6	6	6
	Sub Total:	67%	67%	67%	67%
5 Solve their problem and Take their headache away	10	9	4	4	8
	Sub Total:	90%	40%	40%	80%
6 Price	7	7	4	4	7
	Sub Total:	100%	57%	57%	100%
7 Scalability	8	6	7	7	4
	Sub Total:	75%	88%	88%	50%
8 Make them look good	10	9	5	5	4
	Sub Total:	90%	50%	50%	40%
9 Discreet, supportive and friendly (save face)	10	10	6	4	8
	Sub Total:	100%	60%	40%	80%
10 Whole system approach to solve problem not keep consultant on forever	9	9	5	5	8
	Sub Total:	100%	56%	56%	89%
TOTAL Desirability Score:	92	85	54	51	68

My client's Desirability Rating Score is 85 out of a potential 92, which converts to a percentage of 92 percent. That explains why she is so successful in gaining new business, as well as referrals from extremely satisfied clients.

The idea of course is not to simply shower yourself in glory, but rather to perhaps demonstrate a slightly conservative estimate of your own ability to meet your Ideal Clients Values/Needs/Motivators, and to perhaps be a little generous in respect to your competitors' abilities.

Very often, having applied The Value Slider which confirms Differentiation, we can then confirm Desirability through the Desirability Rating Score. If, however, I find that my client lacks competitive advantage, then we have to go back to The Value Slider and/or re-engineer our ability to meet the Ideal Client's Values/Needs/Motivators.

One of the first mistakes we looked at in the previous section of this book was putting tactics before strategy. I'm hopeful that both The Value Slider and The Desirability Rating will bring to life what I mean by having you ask and answer some of the tough Strategic Questions prior to launching marketing activity.

CHAPTER #2:
THE MARKET

INTRODUCTION

WE ARE REALLY going to drill down on the concept of your Ideal Client, but I will give you three primary characteristics of an Ideal Client before we get into the detail. You can think of this as being like a strategic heads-up before we delve into the tactics of how to put an Ideal Client Profile together.

In bigger picture terms, an Ideal Client has three characteristics:

1. They are already aware of their need for your service.

2. They have the money to pay for your service.

3. The timing in terms of working with you is perfect.

The first characteristic above makes all of your marketing efforts so much easier and more effective. That's because you don't have to go and persuade anyone that what you've got is very cool. This is not to say, necessarily, that an Ideal Client is actively seeking your service, but rather that when they see your service they know they want it.

For example, an Accountant/CPA client of mine has a specialised program that manages and maximises cash flow in a small business. Time and again, research indicates that cash flow is one of the primary concerns of a small business owner. So a business owner may not even be aware that my client's program exists, but when they hear about Scott's program they register an enquiry to find out more because it's a "top of mind" subject.

Another client creates websites in niche industries and selected geographical markets for retailers and tradespeople, then drives traffic to those websites on behalf of the business owner. He sells each website by postcode thereby guaranteeing exclusivity because there is only one website available for each industry per postcode. Essentially, Bruce guarantees to get the phone of the business owner ringing with new customer enquiries. Once again, the owner of the business might be concerned about how he/she will attract new customers, but may not be actively seeking Bruce's solution. But once they hear about Bruce's Value Proposition, they ask for more information and many will go on to buy.

Let's Delve into More Detail

The basis of all effective marketing is covered in this chapter: figuring out *who* you are going to market to, *what* they need, and *where* they hang out.

If you're just starting out, then you're best advised to figure out what's needed and then profile who needs it. However, if you are already established in a specific market, it can work just fine to begin with identifying your Ideal Client Profile first, provided your target market has the ability and willingness to buy your products/service (see the three characteristics above).

For example, a home-based masseur is unlikely to have the ability to invest in a new luxury car, and a male solicitor is unlikely to invest in a course of aromatherapy. This may sound like an obvious point, but I'm still surprised by the number of people who are trying to "milk mice" as I call it by trying to sell to people who can't afford a thing, or simply have no interest in that thing. Better to find a cow. Otherwise, it's painful for the mouse (prospect) and frustrating for you (the milker).

I refer to these two steps as: finding a Specific Unmet Need (SUN) and creating an Ideal Client Profile (ICP); they go together like two wings on the same bird. After we've dealt with these two issues, we'll make sure your marketing focus is crystal clear by identifying what I refer to as your Beachhead.

IDEAL CLIENT PROFILE

In my native country of New Zealand, there once existed a bird called the Moa. Standing up to 2.5 meters tall, the Moa was the world's largest flightless bird. Having no natural predators, it roamed the country in massive numbers, but was eaten to extinction with the arrival of man.

When Europeans arrived, expeditions tried to find any remaining Moas, but failed to do so. Their efforts were said to be hampered by not knowing what a Moa looked like.

What's my point here? If you're going to hunt for a Moa you need to know what a Moa looks like. And it's the same with marketing. If you are going to put a lot of time and effort into your Marketing, make sure that you know exactly what your target prospect looks like, what they like to consume, and where they hang out.

This first part of your Ideal Client Profile is call "demographics" and it's about stating facts that describe your Ideal Client. Another word for demographics in this context might be "who". This is opposed to psychographics which describes the "why" of an Ideal Client's motivators, which we'll deal with a little later.

For example, my Ideal Client Profile is "English speaking business owners who offer a service or advise for a living".

By way of further example, one of my clients who is an executive coach has this Ideal Client Profile: "Top performing managers with problematic social skills". Here's another example that's even more specific: "Women, 40+ years who are renovating their bathroom or kitchen".

When you complete your Ideal Client Profile (ICP), be as specific as you need to be in order to be crystal clear what your Ideal Client looks like. Once you figure out who you are going to target, then you can add their Specific Unmet Need (examples below).

SPECIFIC UNMET NEED (SUN)

Getting this right is the foundation for effective marketing. Once you've identified a need that's not being met, you have a window of opportunity to dominate that market until competitors get wind of your success. In all likelihood, this means you'll have no direct competition for a number of years. Note that the only sustainable competitive advantage is your ability to continually identify unmet needs, and to reinvent your products and services to stay one step ahead of competitors.

Once you've got your first ICP together, then it's time to identify their needs. Questions to ask in relation to your products/services include:

- What do they lie awake worrying about?

- What do they hate having to do?

- What do they hate happening?

- What have they tried, and why didn't it work?

- If they had a magic wand, what would they wish for?

For example, my prospects may lie awake at night worrying about how to get new clients in the door. They hate having to work through complicated planning processes, and they hate spending money on marketing that ends up as wasted money. They may have tried free mentors, or mastermind groups, or business coaches, but none of these things significantly improved their results, probably because the advice they received was ineffective, perhaps because the person they were working with was not a specialist in marketing for the Advisor industry. If they had a magic wand, they'd create a machine that brought new clients into their business every week of the year, including when they were on holiday or at the beach, without them having to cold-call to market or sell.

Can you see how much clarity you will possess, once you've completed that exercise?

Once I have a picture of who my Ideal Clients are and what they need, the marketing campaigns that I put together to attract more of them are infinitely more powerful than any marketing I could do with information that didn't take into account the answers to the above questions.

My web pages, public talks, sales letters, special offers and advertisements all use words which speak to their experiences. Many times after a talk, I've been approached by an audience member who says that my description of them in their business was so accurate that I must have been a fly on the wall of their office.

To reference that further, feel free to refer back to Part One, which is where I established relatability with you by describing your problems and the symptoms of those problems, then painted a picture of what your life would look like when we got your problem to disappear. Again, feel free to refer to Part Two, where I described some of the marketing efforts you have undoubtedly undertaken and why they failed. I could only establish a significant level of credibility, relatability and trust with you because I had clear answers to the above questions prior to writing this book.

And, when you can do the same, you'll discover that many of your prospects are eager to find what you recommend to solve their problems or meet their needs.

In order to get the answers to those questions for your business, the first place to find is "your common sense corner," where you will write down the answers to the above questions based on your own experience.

Go to your favourite café and start to brainstorm the answers to the questions, but don't complicate this! It's often quite straightforward and simple. So if you get answers quickly, don't think that you've necessarily got it wrong.

Other places to find the answers include:

- Frequently expressed frustrations (FEFs) that you've heard from Ideal Clients

- Frequently Asked Questions (FAQs)

And if you don't have enough experience to figure out the answers on your own, or if you want confirmation of your thoughts, then you can dig deeper at these places:

- **www.Amazon.com** — search for top-selling books that relate to your industry and note their titles (this will tell you what's in demand) and customer reviews (this will tell what they liked and sometimes what they thought could be improved)

- **www.Groups.Google.com** — here you'll find a list of on-line forums for almost every subject imaginable. Do some searches for products/services in your industry and note the FEFs and FAQs (see above)

- Industry Association courses and publications — search online for relevant websites and find out what's hot and what's not in regard to 'in demand' courses and articles, and on any online discussions.

- Visit competitors' websites — but a word of caution here: don't assume that they are having any success with what they are doing! A flashy-looking website does not mean new clients are banging down the doors.

- Interview "lost quotes". Get someone to interview people who you thought would become clients but who did not start. Tell the interviewer to assure the people of confidentiality and have them ask, "Why did you choose not to proceed?" and, "What would have had to happen in order for you to proceed". My prediction is that this will prove to be one of the most valuable exercises you'll ever undertake.

- Buy the magazines that your Ideal Clients buy, that are related to your industry, and see what's been advertised; read the letters to the editor and note Frequently Expressed Frustrations and FAQs.

ESTABLISHING YOUR BEACHHEAD

Lastly, decide where you'll concentrate your focus.

The metaphor I use for this is the concept of a "Beachhead". By way of illustration, when the Allies invaded France to liberate Western Europe from the Nazis, they selected five beaches on the coast of Normandy France to establish their initial Beachheads. They dominated those places prior to pushing further inland.

It can be very difficult when starting out, and sometimes impossible to succeed, without first picking some form of niche to focus on. For your first Beachhead, you get to choose from one or more of three aspects:

1. A product/service niche

2. An industry niche

3. A regional niche

Establishing a Beachhead is a metaphor for focusing your resources on a small part of a large market. The idea is to dominate that niche prior to expansion. That means getting your Lead Generation systems working well, getting the Lead Conversion system working well, and getting Value Delivery systems working well — and doing all of that in a highly profitable manner.

The Beachhead concept is sometimes a very difficult one for my new clients to buy into, because I'm asking them to initially limit their vision and focus to a small area. By contrast, an entrepreneur's vision for invading Western Europe would have been something like this: "Okay, let's take France on Sunday, Belgium and Holland, Monday, and Germany, Tuesday ... or maybe Wednesday"!

Remember, in respect to the time for expansion, an army would not attempt to break out of the beachhead until it knew that supply lines and other logistical systems were functioning and could support the expansion. Ditto with your business; you must ensure that any systems that you need in place to grow your business are functioning well, prior to breaking out of your Beachhead.

Key point: any weakness in marketing or support systems will be magnified when you expand, so make sure your "supply lines" (including marketing and product/service supply) are up to the task prior to expanding. The cracks only get bigger when you expand!

As mentioned above, you can choose from one or two of three niches to start with. Either a Service niche and/or an Industry Sector niche and/or a Regional niche.

But let's debunk a major myth, which is that in order to succeed you *must* niche in a specific industry or sector, which is not always the case.

For example, in 1995 I launched the Entrepreneur's Success Program, which was a three-year, curriculum-based program for business owners. It plugged a gap in the market (SUN) for the education of entrepreneurs. It was holistic (work/life balance and more) and free of irrelevant assignments and mumbo-jumbo (think "MBA").

I took the business international and in the first seven years we not only had clients from multiple regions, but also from some 97 different industries. As you can see, we niched the service and region (we started in one city only) but we had no industry niche. Once we were established as the dominant player in the first city, we expanded to others and then overseas.

Similarly, my colleague Mike O'Hagan started "Mini-Movers" with a spare pick-up truck and $200. He hired a driver to move small lots — e.g. a kitchen table — from one side of the city to another. After growing the business and dominating the small lot removal business in his city, he then expanded to other cities and expanded his range of services to include household lots. That's the metaphorical equivalent of an army breaking out from a beachhead.

So, do you *need* to niche? Well, yes. But not necessarily in an industry or sector. You may niche in a specific service. But either way, remember the Beachhead principle: focus resources on a small part of a large market, dominate it and then expand. You can expand either your target market and/or your Service range and/or your region.

The "small part" referred to above has to be large enough to satisfy your short-term revenue objectives (at least), but allow for expansion once established. So while the colleague I referred to previously was successful in starting swimming schools for "Little People", he would have struggled if he had targeted "Little People who were blind in their left eye and had a bad lisp" ☺.

The last word on niching in an industry is this: while it's not necessary to target an industry niche, but it is generally easier and more effective. So if you have experience in an industry niche (e.g. you were a chiropractor or a vehicle designer or professional sailor) and that industry is large enough for you to become established in, then by all means target a specific industry. Just don't assume that an industry niche will *automatically* make marketing more successful. It's always "test and measure".

Case Study

To illustrate the focus that the Beachhead concept brings to a business owner, I'll share a conversation I recently had with two new clients. And this is typical of many new clients.

Their business is run by two people and has three service offerings:

Face-to-face clinic visits for counselling

Group courses offering advanced Kinesiology training for Kinesiologists

Online relationships training courses

My clients are highly intelligent people and the main service provider is probably a genius. However, even he was struggling with the complexity of attempting to grow these three different business areas simultaneously. Not enough time and not enough mental space (the latter being more important than the former).

And so I asked which of the three areas offered the *best* opportunity for fast and profitable growth.

After he answered that it was the clinic work, we agreed that whatever was going to happen with the other two areas would have to happen organically until we had clinic visits to the point where the cash flow was such that he could breathe easy and could afford to begin to bring in contractors to take over some of the workload.

Next, I asked about the types of clients who came into the clinic, and we isolated three separate markets:

1. Counselling services to individuals and couples who want to shift from emotional pain to freedom.

2. Educational services for 8- to10-year-old school children with learning difficulties.

3. Relief from back and other body pain.

Again, the complexity of developing three different Marketing Messages and multiple campaigns for each group is something that would daunt even a marketing Einstein.

And so after more chatting, we picked #2 above, because that market has proved to be the most responsive and easiest to access and also was very profitable.

What a difference! We went from the equivalent of recapturing Europe, Asia and Africa before lunchtime to securing just the one beach!

Putting It All Together

Your next step is to combine your Ideal Client Profile, their Specific Unmet Need, and your Beachhead into one succinct statement. Tip: You are better to sacrifice completeness for memorability. In other words: keep it short.

By way of example, here's some Product/Service niche examples that include some Regional niches and some Industry niches, along with ICP and SUNs (all real businesses):

- Fly fishing therapy for breast cancer victims in Montana who appreciate that nature offers a gentle and enjoyable way of recovery.

- Ten-minute haircuts for busy female executives in Hong Kong who need a good cut cheap and fast.

- Small-lot removals from one side of town to another in Brisbane for people who want someone else to take the hassle out of shifting stuff.

- Asian bamboo varieties on the Sunshine Coast for gardeners who want something different.

- Organic medicinal honey for health-conscious females in Japan who care about health and who appreciate beautiful packaging.

- Three-way suspension seats for military attack boats and other high-speed craft for sailors who want to stay injury-free on the high seas.

- Vintage beach shack furniture for laid back surfing families in Noosa who appreciate fashion from the 50s and 60s.Solar power installation in Dakota for large-scale manufacturers.

- Out-of-court divorce settlement services in Australia for parents who want a low cost and amicable settlement that puts the children first.

- Fair trade, organic Ecuadorian Coffee beans in the United Kingdom for sustainably minded metrosexuals and other ecologically hip dudes.

- Organic (Free Range ☺) Cherry tomatoes for cooks who want the sweetest, freshest and most nutritious tomatoes.

- Scottish landlords with multiple properties who want economical and hassle-free property management.

- Australian business owners with revenue of 1 million or more who want simple but proven ways to get more clients.

- Stay-at-home mothers in California who want to generate a five-figure income annually while investing less than 25 hours per week.

- Fast-food restaurant owners in Hong Kong who want to increase profit without working harder.

- Pet owners who appreciate super friendly service as well as professional animal health care.

If you want to further refine your statement, then use the chart on the right, from one of my training courses. The more of these characteristics you can tick, the more likely your success when you start marketing.

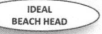

The intersection of...

✓ Love-ability (passion)

✓ Slice-ability (small niche/large market)

✓ Specific-ability (unmet needs)

✓ Fulfil-ability (to meet needs)

✓ Pay-ability (client can/will)

✓ Reach-ability (marketing, distribution)

✓ Profit-ability (positive sale/margin ratio)

✓ Scale-ability (can expand, leverage)

CHAPTER #3:
THE MESSAGE

ALMOST UNIVERSALLY, THE clients I work with tell me that creating a Marketing Message that generates enquiries is the toughest thing that they have ever tried to do.

I like that. And the reason is simple: Many clients have told me that I'm pretty darned good at it so it helps me to Be In Demand. I may be lousy at a lot of things, but words are my forte.

Having blown my own trumpet (probably just a tad too loudly) I'll now attempt to justify my claim to fame.

This chapter will reveal what I believe to be the most concise, yet comprehensive guide to creating a Marketing Message that generates fresh, inbound, highly qualified enquiries from potential new Ideal Clients.

Big call! Let's see if I can deliver.

Just as in the previous chapter, I'm going to start with a big-picture look at the characteristics in this case of an effective Marketing Message. Then I'll go on to share more detail with you, including breakthrough methods and concepts such as The Dinner Party Question, The Intersection and The Waterfall. Hold onto your hat!

Three primary characteristics of an effective Marketing Message are as follows:

1. It's benefit-rich

2. It's differentiated

3. It contains specifics

Being Benefit-Rich is the most important of these three characteristics.

Differentiation is not enough on its own, but it's super important because it adds more power to the stated Benefit. That's because differentiation is the thing that most creates "cut through" in the marketplaces and makes the Marketing Message highly noticeable.

Unlike differentiation, the inclusion of specifics is not super important. However, when it can be added it further enhances the power of the stated Benefit. Note that "specifics" will normally include some form of number such as a dollar amount or a percentage and quite often a duration. You'll see this come to life when we look at the Dinner Party Question below.

By the way, what I refer to as a Marketing Message you may have heard described as a unique selling proposition or an elevator pitch. Regardless of the label we give it, its objective is the same: to elicit an enquiry. And as you'll see shortly, my concept of a Marketing Message goes way beyond unique selling propositions or elevator pitches.

A big mistake that people make in crafting a Marketing Message is to describe what they do or their service. It's the cart before the horse. Most people could not give a dime (or "one brass razoo" as we say here Australia) about what you do, how you do it, whether you are passionate about it, how long you been doing it for, who you've done it with, where you do it, how much it costs, or what your website looks like. That is, not until they know what's in it for them. Then they care about that other stuff, but not before.

THE DINNER PARTY QUESTION

This concept is not only the perfect way to illustrate how an effective Marketing Message is constructed using the three characteristics mentioned above, it also serves as my litmus test for whether or not we've got the Marketing Message right.

I'll now introduce Max, who is a client of mine. Max's company develops Point of Sale (POS) software for fast food restaurants, the latter being known in the industry as "Quick Service Restaurants" or "QSRs".

Let's imagine that Max is fortuitously sitting at a dinner party next to someone who owns eight McDonald's restaurant outlets and we'll call that someone Pam. So Pam's had a glass or two of red wine and she's telling Max all about her eight restaurants and how she keeps buying more restaurants. But she adds that she is incredibly frustrated because she can't figure out how to increase the sales within each restaurant, let alone how to increase profit margins, which is why she keeps buying new outlets.

Pam goes on for some time about her problems of lack of revenue and profit growth before she realises she is potentially being a bit of a bore (not true in this case because Max is set to pounce) and so she turns to Max and says "I'm sorry Max. I've been so rude, I've been telling you all about my problems at work ... what is it that you do?"

Now, prior to working on his Marketing Message, Max would have responded with something like *"well it's funny that you ask because I develop POS software for QSRs".*

At this point Pam's eyes would glaze over and she'd mumble something like "that's nice " and proceed to reach for the bottle of red wine, all along thinking to herself *"OMG this guy is about to try and flog me some software"."*.

Contrast that to Max's response *after* we worked on Max's Marketing Message.

After being asked what he does for a living, Max would respond with *"it's funny that you ask because I increase the sales and profits in QSRs by 25% or more within 90 days".*

Now if you were the owner of those eight restaurants and *you* were stressed about flat-lining revenue and profitability, what would *your* response be? I'd bet you dollars to doughnuts that you would put your glass of wine down and lean in a little closer to Max and ask *"how do you do that?".* And that being the case, we would have just generated a lead.

Now let's run our marketing slide rule over Max's Marketing Message and see to what extent it contained the three characteristics identified at the start of this chapter.

Is Max's Marketing Message benefit-rich? Absolutely!

Is his Marketing Message differentiated from that of his competitors? You betcha! Because his competitors blather on about software, not about the benefits of this software.

Does this Marketing Message contains specifics? Bingo! 25 percent within 90 days is very specific.

Furthermore, following my recommendation, Max also was prepared to offer a guarantee of results. Now that's what I call an irresistible offer.

This is very similar to another client of mine, Wayne. A brilliant physiotherapist who discovered that the cause of many workplace injuries stemmed from people performing a repetitive task using the same muscle set over and over. Wayne developed a re-training method to eliminate that cause. He can now promote his methodology through the Marketing Message: *"we guarantee to eliminate 75% of workplace injuries within 90 days"*.

You'll note again that Wayne's Marketing Message is benefit-rich, is differentiated, and it contains specifics. If Wayne was sitting at a dinner party with the CEO of a large manufacturing company and he/she asked Wayne what he did for a living and he responded with *"we guarantee to eliminate 75% of workplace injuries within 90 days"* then that CEO would have to be brain-dead not to ask him more about his service.

THE INTERSECTION

This concept is extremely powerful because it shows you very simply and yet incredibly accurately exactly what good marketing is all about.

In the previous chapter I mentioned that at a strategic level there were three primary characteristics of an **Ideal Client** which were:

1. They are already aware of their need for your service.

2. They have the money to pay for your service.

3. The timing in terms of working with you is perfect.

And I'm sure it will be fresh in your memory that the three primary characteristics of an effective **Marketing Message** are

1. It's benefit rich

2. It's differentiated

3. It contains specifics

Now that we've established those characteristics we can set them together on a collision course and reveal The Intersection:

Effective marketing is summed up in the above image. You will

generate fresh, high-quality, inbound new client enquiries when you intersect your potential Ideal Client with your effective Marketing Message.

In respect to "Specifics", bear in mind that it's not *always* possible to include specifics in a Marketing Message and it is also not critical to do so. But if you are able to include specifics then it will certainly add the power of believability to your Marketing Message.

Unfortunately, Ideal Clients don't walk around with a sign on the forehead. So what that means is we often have to get our Marketing Message in front of a group of potential Ideal Clients. We'll cover more on that in Chapter 4 of this part when we look at the most effective Marketing Mediums to push your Marketing Message through.

THE WATERFALL

An effective Marketing Message doesn't stop with the benefit rich, differentiated statement that contains specifics. It starts there.

Your Marketing Message is *everything* that the marketplace and your Ideal Clients see or hear prior to buying, and also during the Value Delivery process.

This therefore includes but is not limited to testimonials/case studies, guarantees, trademarks, lead magnets such as special reports, your book, your webinar, a talk that you give, a pre-client engagement consult, your core service (which is also a part of your marketing arsenal because it can generate more sales to the same client or gain referrals to new clients) any back-end services you offer (more on that in chapter 5 to follow), your business card, your tradeshow banner, your LinkedIn profile, your blog, your podcasts, your articles, your business Facebook page and absolutely everything else that engage your target market and Ideal Clients.

If you change your Marketing Message between the dinner party conversation and the follow-up pre-engagement meeting with the prospective client you met at your dinner party then you will be in danger of losing that prospect.

A short story to illustrate my point.

For decades now I've been a big fan of Bob Dylan. In the unlikely event that you've been living under a rock for the last 50 years, I'll explain who he is. Bob Dylan started out as a folk singer, singing protest songs about the Vietnam War in the 1960s. His repertoire of protest songs was a hallmark of the flower power generation.

His first tour to Great Britain and Europe sold out months ahead of the gigs. The media were swarming all over young Bobby and tens of thousands of excited fans greeted him whenever and wherever his plane touched down.

But the tour was anything but a success.

The reason was simple: Bob Dylan had moved on from singing folk/protest songs and had chosen his first overseas tour to introduce a new repertoire of rock songs.

His fans hated this so much and felt such a sense of betrayal that at some concerts they took tomatoes and rotten eggs and used them and Bob Dylan for target practice.

Why did so many previously besotted and idolising fans suddenly turn their back on Bob Dylan?

The answer is that they wanted to keep hearing the same message from Bob.

The moral of the story is this, and you would benefit greatly to take note:

So don't have one message at the dinner party, another on your business card, another embedded in the title of your webinar, a different one again in the title of your book, or indeed fail to embed the message somewhere in your pre-engagement client Consult.

Effective politicians do this repetition of the message during election campaigns. They'll repeat the same message — typically two or three points, no more — over and over again ad nauseam. In the last election here in Australia, the successful candidate for the Prime Minister's job was like a broken record saying over and again *"We'll scrap the carbon tax, end the waste, stop the boats and build the infrastructure of the 21st century"*. If he had failed to repeat the message continually throughout his election campaign, I have no doubt whatsoever that his party would have received fewer votes.

The Waterfall is a metaphor that I created to remind you of the critical need to align the message that's embedded in your Marketing Message through all marketing elements, including the services that you provide, which clearly must deliver on the promise contained in your Marketing Message. Here is a visual from one of my courses to further reinforce the point of alignment:

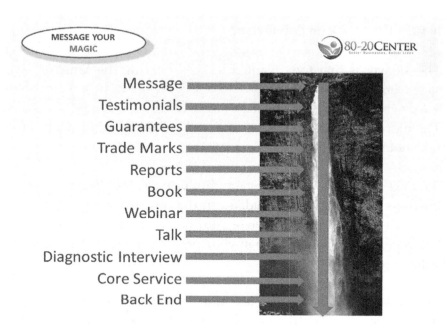

And here's what most business owners do with their waterfall:

The above image represents the inconsistency of the Marketing Message promoted by 99.9 percent of Advisors and explains why even those who have a semi-effective Marketing Message failed to cut through in the marketplace.

THE BOOK COVER

In Chapter 1 of this part, I wrote about the Book Cover versus the Book, the former being the perception of what you do and the latter being the reality of what you do.

The concept of the Book Cover is integral to your Marketing Message because people will judge your Book/Service by its cover.

So as part of exploring your Marketing Message, we also need to look at what's on your book cover.

There are five methods to enhance your Book Cover. Note that a failure to include *each* of these five methods will dilute your capability for Being In Demand.

Book Cover Enhancement #1: Professional Image

Because we know that people will judge a Book by its Cover, it's essential that the book cover is a fair reflection of the content of the book.

While is not exactly a Book Cover, the sign on the right illustrates the point. When you look at the sign, what do you automatically assume about the quality of the meat sold by Strongs? Most probably you would go somewhere else for your meat despite the fact that the words on the sign declare boldly that Strongs has "best quality" meat.

What this tells us is that the image portrayed is more important than the words spoken. Therefore — assuming that you want to attract high-quality, premium priced clients — it's clearly of critical importance that the image you project is highly professional.

This applies to the image portrayed by your website (please, please, please resist the temptation to ask your 14-year-old who is doing a school project on websites to build you one), your LinkedIn profile (make sure it doesn't resemble an abandoned house and that it has a professional photo of yourself displayed rather than a selfie), whether or not your shoes are shined, how clean your offices are, how you set up a room for a training or coaching session, the clarity and crispness and visual appeal of your logo, how clean your car is, how well-dressed you are and so on.

With offshoring, professional-looking websites, logos and other graphics can be created for a matter of hundreds of dollars, so there really isn't any excuse these days to have anything less than a professional image. See websites such as **www.upwork.com, www.guru.com, www.freelancer.com** and more.

Book Cover Enhancement #2: Proprietary Terminology
When you trademark a certain term, you immediately eliminate all direct competitors. For example, only my client Tess has registered "Cohesive Conversations" as a trademark.

Tess is a giant and a genius in the world of effective communication. The problem was that her Book Cover — the perception the marketplace had of her work — was similar to many of her competitors. I know that the clients she brought on board absolutely loved her, because on many occasions they would fly her around the country repeatedly, paying premium-priced fees, to have her engage with an organization's most important senior executives.

So because she is a genius at what she does, once she gets a client on board she is away laughing. The problem, like many of my other new clients have, was not what happened once she was in front of a prospective Ideal Client. Rather, it was *getting in front of the prospective Ideal Client..*

Naturally, we worked on differentiating her Marketing Message, and as a part of that I recommended that she coin the phrase Cohesive Communication and register a trademark for that phrase.

Now, when someone reads a book or attends one of her presentations, and they get hot and frothy about the benefit of Cohesive Communication in their workplace and enjoying all of the engagement and productivity benefits that come out of that, who are they going to call? Tess, of course! Because she's the only one who has Cohesive Communication.

Previously, when Tess was pitching for business she was, metaphorically speaking, standing in the middle of the country among hundreds, if not thousands, of other communication experts, all with a hand up saying "Pick Me!".

Now when Tess presents a proposal to a prospective client, it's like she's standing on her own little island with all of her competitors still standing back on the mainland begging to be chosen. If someone wants what Tess has, then they are going to have to go to her island because she is the only one on it.

So, create a cool name that describes your program/course/service and register it with the government so that only you can use that term.

Now, I'm not a trademark specialist so I can't advise you about what you can and cannot register as a trademark, other than to say that, if you use words that are in common daily usage, you are unlikely to be able to register that as a trademark unless you present it in a unique form with a unique image.

For example, here's a term I registered for my Lead Generation Planning And Implementation tool called Command+Control:

 COMMAND+CONTROL®

While I can't register the words Command+Control as a trademark, but I can register the words and logo together in the form of an image.

You can overdo this, but I've rarely seen it done. Most Advisors have zero registered intellectual property, and that means their Book Cover appears to be undifferentiated from competitors.

Book Cover Enhancement #3: Pricing

I covered the subject of premium pricing in Chapter 12, Part Two so I won't go into detail here, other than to say that if you ensure that you are at the top end of the pricing range you will be far more likely to be perceived (Book Cover) as having a premium service.

However, premium pricing isn't all there is to the subject of pricing. You can also segment the payment of your fee so it becomes far easier for prospective Ideal Clients to say yes.

Let's say you have a service that involved consulting and training and the price tag was $50,000. You can break down the whole service into a few series of phases, price each one individually, and make sure each phase was self-contained in regard to value. Then if a client decided to stop after the first phase they could do so and still have received full value from the service for that phase.

Furthermore, you can provide a guarantee, of either performance or satisfaction, to further differentiate yourself from competitors and also mitigate the risk in the mind of your prospect.

You'll find that even most corporate clients will care about how they cash flow your fee, that is how much they have to pay you each month, more than they care about the total size of the fee itself. I learned this from the vehicle industry decades ago: most people only want to know how much the deposit is and how much they pay each month. Most people (sure, not all of them) don't even add up the total they are paying on a finance deal; they just look at the monthly payment and figure out if they can afford it.

Finally, on the subject of pricing as it applies to premium priced services: never, ever, ever…discount. You destroy the perception of having a premium service if you stoop to discounting and you also destroy the psychology that I'm going to share with you in the next enhancement. Note that there is a place for discounting, but not when it comes to services that you want to be thought of as premium quality.

Book Cover Enhancement #4: Reverse Psychology

Maxwell Maltz (1889–1975) was an American cosmetic surgeon and author of the best-selling book *Psycho-Cybernetics,* which contained a series of concepts and techniques for improving a person's self-image and self-esteem. Maltz was probably *the* father of the modern day self-help movement and his books also made a major contribution to our understanding of how the unconscious mind works.

Psycho-Cybernetics is a classic and can still be bought on **www.amazon.com** today, more than 50 years after it was first published. Suffice it to say that Maltz knew a thing or two about human psychology.

Maltz tells the story of when he opened his first surgery. He'd rented an office, bought furniture and expensive surgical equipment, installed a phone line and hired a receptionist. When everything was set up and ready to go, he proudly hung out his bronze plaque: "Dr. M. Maltz. M.D. F.C.I.S."

Then he and his receptionist sat and waited for the phone to ring. And they waited, and waited, and waited … for weeks. All the time Maltz was watching his meager bank balance diminish even further with every passing week.

When the first prospect finally called and asked for an appointment, Maltz had his exceedingly bored receptionist fully trained and ready to leap into action.

As per instructions, she firstly let the phone ring seven times. When she finally answered it she made sure that her voice sounded professional but brisk, as if she were in a hurry. Then when the caller asked for an appointment with Maltz, the receptionist made a point of ensuring that the caller could hear the pages turning in her diary. The caller was then informed that Dr. Maltz would see him/her in two weeks' time.

This, despite the fact that, at that point, the diary was completely empty and Maltz was next to broke.

The reason that Maltz always booked clients two weeks out was three-fold.

Firstly, it gave the client the impression that Maltz was so much in demand that it took two weeks to get in to see him. Clearly this was an erroneous impression to give at the time of launching his business; I presume that his strategy was "fake it until you make it".

Secondly, the client kept the appointment because they thought that if they cancelled, it was going to take at least another two weeks to get back in.

Finally, Maltz knew that a client would value and desire his services far more if he was just a shade more unobtainable than other specialists, and that meant he could also charge higher prices.

What Maltz was exploiting was what I can only describe as a somewhat bizarre characteristic of humankind: the thing we want more than anything else is *the thing that we may not be able to have*. And often, even if we don't really need it.

Reverse Psychology is defined as motivating a person to do what you want them to do by asking them to do the opposite. For example, if you have a young child playing inside and you want them to go outside, you tell them that they are not allowed to go outside. In the majority of cases, the child will protest and then you can "relent" and allow them to go outside to play. Mission accomplished, via Reverse Psychology.

On a similar note, if you appear to be easy to get, then prospective clients will develop apathy towards you. Likewise, if you appear to be able to start at any time, clients will develop an apathy towards you. Which leads us nicely into the next enhancement.

Book Cover Enhancement #5: Scarcity

One of the most oft-utilized forms of increasing demand is limiting supply, and this of course immediately increases any pre-existing desire for the product.

Scarcity is easy for most business owners to utilize and yet it's also very powerful. However, to be clear: scarcity on its own will have zero effect on a buyer unless there is a pre-existing want or need.

For example: having just fitted a new set of tyres to my car, no amount of "limited-time-special" offers will have the slightest effect in terms of increasing my desire to buy more tyres because that need has already been satisfied.

If, however, I was in need of new tyres, then an advertisement offering a savings of 20 percent for a limited time would greatly influence me. If you've been paying attention, as I'm sure you have, then you'll note that I've previously discouraged you from offering discounts for premium products; I'm simply illustrating the point that limited time offers increase demand.

Scarcity is mostly manipulated by the seller. For example, USA motorcycle manufacturer Harley Davidson has a deliberate policy of underproduction. At the risk of oversimplifying their strategy, they estimate how many motorcycles will be in demand for any given year and then produce less than that number, thus maintaining an extraordinarily high level of brand desirability.

Not to mention premium prices compared to most other motor-cycle manufacturers. (At time of this writing, they have other issues which are adversely affecting their market share. But that has more to do with their failure to realign the Harley brand outside of post-menopausal baby boomer men who, on the weekend, swap their suit and tie for leather and studs and become bad ass pretenders.)

Here's a list of some ways that scarcity can be employed:

- Regular limited availability (e.g. the Harley Davidson example above)

- Ad Hoc limited availability ("only while stocks last")

- Special price for a limited time ("this weekend only")

- Bonus offered for the first [x number] ordered

- Bonus offered for a limited time ("hurry and order now to claim your free [xyz]"

- Limited edition offers ("100 copies only, personally signed by the author")

- Collector's edition e.g. 12 editions, one sent each month ("get the complete set")

- Auctions ("going … going … gone!")

- Advertising, event or publication deadlines

- "Early Bird" discounts or bonuses

- End of financial year sale (effective on business items to quickly claim tax deductibility)

Many years ago, I experimented with an offer at the end of a webinar that I had previously run regularly.

Over the first series of webinars, I presented the offer, which was for my Killer Referrals Machine program at a very special price. I told attendees they had 48 hours to order at the special price and that the offer would then expire. The take-up rate was positive and I was moderately happy with the results.

Then I ran exactly the same webinar, but inserted a bonus for all those who bought within 20 minutes. After I explained the special offer price for the Killer Referrals Machine program, I then displayed the following slide:

I then also displayed a countdown timer which started at 20 minutes and ticked away at the top of the screen while I took questions.

20 Minute Fast Action Reward

For ANY order: "Success University"

- 25 priceless MP3 hours of some of the best business building advice available on the market today

- Introducing over 100 proven business growth ideas, all in one place. A real value packed investment

- Instant access to all PLUS one a month drip feed system

- Sells for AU$475 – yours FREE with ANY order in next 20 min

Hidden URL: www.8020center.com/Referrals/

I further explained that the reason I was creating this limited time offer was that I knew that many people would benefit greatly from my program and I wanted to encourage them to make a decision now rather than leave it to later and possibly get distracted and forget about it. In other words I gave them what they needed to make a decision now: a valid reason.

The introduction of a scarcity-based bonus increased my sales on average by 27 percent. The inclusion of the countdown timer brought a sense of urgency to the offer, and it worked well because I also explained in rational and logical terms why I was doing it.

By way of further example, I've noticed that if I hold a four-day sale for a specific product, the last day of the sale produces an additional 50 percent of the sales over and above the total of the first three days. In other words, over a four-day sale period, if I sell 100 items on the first three days then I can normally expect to sell another 50 on the last day.

And it's the same with event registrations. If I send out three email invitations to attend a webinar, I always send the last one on the day prior to the event. Registrations on that day are always roughly an additional 50 percent of the total from the previous two invites. The fact that a deadline is about to expire motivates some people to make a decision that they were not prepared to make earlier.

Here's the bottom line: you will be more in demand when you limit supply or when you give the perception that supply is limited.

CHAPTER #4:
THE MEDIUMS

MARKETING **M**EDIUMS **HAS** nothing to do with hiring a psychic or consulting Ouija boards to see where you should direct your marketing efforts. If only it were that simple.

Think of a Marketing Medium as a channel through which you can be pushing your Marketing Message.

I've previously commented on the fact that some mediums are better suited to specific products/services than others. For example, smart retailers can do very well by advertising physical products through newspapers, magazines, radio and television.

WHY PRINT, RADIO AND TELEVISION MEDIUMS ARE MOSTLY A WASTE OF MONEY FOR ADVISORS

Last year I had the head of a national association of professional Advisors ask me to consult with them on how they should spend their $120,000 marketing budget. Their draft marketing plan was put together by the national committee, which consisted of regionally elected representatives from each state and territory. Therefore the committee consisted of a group of highly qualified, highly skilled and highly professional Advisors. As impressive as this committee was, it naturally contained no professional marketers. Being the smart people that they were, they recognised this and asked for my opinion.

When I reviewed their draft marketing plan, it wasn't surprising to discover that they were planning to invest their $120,000 in print and radio media. My initial reaction was to suggest to them that, if they wish to proceed with the plan's current form, they would be better off if they took $60,000 and flushed it down the toilet and kept the other $60,000 in the bank. I explained that this approach would leave them much better off than if they invested the $120,000 in print and radio media.

There are a couple of reasons for this. Firstly, if a larger organisation is going to undertake print and radio media, it needs to be a very long-term commitment to get the brand embedded in the brains of the buyers. The likes of McDonald's and Coca-Cola have what is referred to as "Share of Mind" because of their relentless advertising campaigns.

Share of Mind means that their brand is the first one that comes to mind when the products they sell are mentioned in generic terms. For example, if I say "fast food" most people immediately think of McDonald's. If I say "soft drink," most people immediately think of Coca-Cola. And this one may change now, but those in my generation would respond to "safe car" with Volvo.

So the first reason why print, radio and television are ineffective and a waste of money for professional services and Advisors to push their Marketing Message through is that we simply don't have the budgets of some of the large corporate brands I've just mentioned. We can't sustain marketing campaigns that transcend years, let alone decades and that is what you need to do if you want to be effective in gaining Share of Mind.

The second reason is that when people are looking for professional advice or a professional service, they prefer to find an Advisor through a referral from a trusted colleague or friend. If that's not possible, then they need to have some form of sample experience with the Advisor prior to hiring.

The reason is that when I buy a car or smartphone or a computer, I'm not entering into a human relationship with that thing. But when I hire an Advisor, it's a little bit like getting married.

We start a relationship and there is often a honeymoon period filled with excitement and anticipation, and then that dissipates and we have to learn to work with each other, navigating the million subtle variables in our personalities, expectations, beliefs, values, vision and so on.

And if we can't get a referral to an Advisor, then we want to experience that person prior to engagement. We can gain that "getting to know you" experience by reading their book, by attending an event where they present, or listening to them being interviewed. Without that experience, hiring an Advisor from a phone book would be like getting married *before* the first date.

The chances of having a successful relationship with an Advisor based on an advertisement are about the same as a blind squirrel finding an acorn in a forest. It does happen, but it's pretty rare.

It's worth noting an exception to the above, which is when marketing an event through radio or print media, as opposed to marketing your services, can be very worthwhile and highly profitable.

THE MARKETING STOOL

There are four Marketing Mediums that I recommend to Advisors for pushing their Marketing Message through so that it reaches their Ideal Client (see The Intersection in Chapter 3 above) and each of these four represents a leg on a four-legged stool. The seat on the stool represents my OPN strategy, which creates an inexhaustible supply of leads to each of the legs. More on OPN later.

Before we delve into the four recommended Marketing Mediums, it's worthwhile first to reflect on the characteristics of the ideal Marketing Medium/Lead Generator/Lead Source.

By way of introduction to the subject I have two quick questions to ask you.

Question one is: "What have you been told that you should be doing for your marketing?"

Chances are that the answers will be many and varied. Article marketing, interviews, podcasts, Facebook, Twitter, LinkedIn, Instagram, Pinterest, free e-books, blogging, telemarketing, cold calling, referral campaigns, search engine optimisation, pay-per-click and probably much more.

If you are typical of the thousands of people that I've asked this question when I'm speaking to conferences or other groups, then several things may have happened in respect to your marketing attempts.

Because you receive such varied advice from *many* people who confidently proclaim that their particular specialty (blogging or podcasting or LinkedIn or article marketing and so on) is the answer, and then ask you to invest in their course/program, you're probably very confused and simply don't know where to start.

In multiple surveys that I've run over the years, more than 97 percent of business owners state that they want a higher flow of new clients than they are currently getting. Add to that fact that more than 80 percent of Advisors spend less than one hour a week on marketing and you end up with a real head scratcher: if such an overwhelming number of Advisors want new clients, then why the heck are they undertaking little or no marketing activity?

The answer is certainly not that they are stupid or lazy. The majority of Advisors that I've met are smart and hard-working. It's simply that they are a specialist at whatever it is they do as opposed to being a specialist at marketing whatever it is they do.

My conclusion is that Advisors are failing to undertake marketing activity either because they are completely confused by so much conflicting and diversified advice in respect to how and where to do the marketing, or that they have actually followed the advice of all the people selling programs and courses but have very little, if anything, to show for it.

Can you relate to one of those reasons? If so, then I strongly recommend you pay particular attention to Chapter 6 in this part of the book with special reference to The First Domino, The Gold Standard and revisit The Poland Weekly Calendar.

Question two is: "on a scale of 1 to 10, with 1 being "sucks" and 10

being "I'm knocking it out of the ballpark", how is that working for you so far?"

If you answered somewhere between one and three then you are again typical of the thousands of people that have responded to that question during one of my presentations on Lead Generation.

I've touched on a couple of reasons already why Advisors are failing to persist in their attempts to generate leads proactively: most people aren't actively marketing either because they are frozen like a deer in front of a car's headlights by the overwhelming diversity and sometimes contradictory advice of self-proclaimed marketing gurus, or they implemented the latter's advice and it didn't work so the Advisor gives up.

However, there is a third reason why Advisors who want a regular flow of more clients failed to undertake marketing activity. Sometimes the advice they receive is so comprehensive and complicated that it's difficult to implement, and rather than work through that particular headache, it's far easier to find something simpler such as clearing emails.

Therefore, whatever Marketing Mediums you choose, you must be able to undertake them by following a simple, proven, step-by-step process that you can be walked through, hand-in-hand, by an experienced, successful guide/mentor.

It just happens to be a fact that when developing a new skill we need a teacher of some description.

To overcome the unlikely but possible idea in your mind that I'm recommending you find a marketing teacher simply out of self-promotional interest, I'd invite you to reflect for a moment on what would happen if one of your potential Ideal Clients read a book that you wrote about your specialty and then attempted to implement your advice on their own.

I suspect that you'll agree with me that they would most likely mess it up simply because they don't have your years and possibly decades of experience.

It would be a bit like taking someone who's lived in a remote Amazonian tribe all their life, putting him in a car parked on the side of the freeway with a manual on how to drive and asking him to head off down the freeway. Despite the fact that our Amazonian friend has read the "how-to manual" on driving, the exercise will end in tears, and possibly worse.

Having got that out of the way, let's have a look at…

TEN CHARACTERISTICS OF THE PERFECT MARKETING MEDIUM

1. Produces high-*quality* , well-qualified leads

2. Highly *affordable*

3. Relatively *easy*

4. Relatively *simple*

5. *Scalable* (one to many)

6. Feels *natural*, organic, no "selling" required

7. National and *global* potential

8. *Automated* (can generate leads when you're asleep or on holiday)

9. Provides an exceptionally *high ROI* (return on investment)

10. "Rinse and *repeat*"

I have presented the above list to audiences many times and to date I don't think I've had anyone suggest another characteristic, so my conclusion is that it's a fairly comprehensive list.

And I think that you'll agree that if you had a Marketing Medium that generated leads and ticked all the above boxes, then you'd be pretty happy about that, right?

By contrast, Marketing Mediums that suck include anything that relies on a High Flow Model (see Marketing Mistake #4 from Part Two of this book), expensive advertising, a broad approach to Social Media (not targeted enough to generate leads), cold calling (soul destroying and ineffective) and anything that takes too long and/or too much time to generate the leads. The latter includes article marketing, blogging, podcasts and the like. That's not to say they have no place in our Marketing Stool, but it's not where I recommend you start. (More on that later)

MARKETING LEG #1: WEBINARS

One Marketing Medium that ticks all 10 ideal characteristics is a webinar and we'll look at the reasons why in a moment. But first of all, a caveat: like all Marketing Mediums, webinars can be effective or ineffective lead generators depending on whether you know what you're doing or not.

A big mistake a lot of trainers and other presenters make is thinking they can construct a webinar that's being run for the purpose of generating leads (what I call a "marketing webinar") in the same fashion as a webinar that's being run for the purpose of training.

If you run a marketing webinar like you run a training webinar, you have a bunch of people who are happy to have attended, but think they can successfully implement the information you have given them on their own.

And of course, 95 percent of them will get distracted with something else and will therefore never get around to implementing. And the 5 percent that do attempt to implement will most likely mess it up because they simply don't have your experience and expertise.

Another big mistake that's made is presenting a webinar in the same way that someone

Presents a seminar or workshop. The reason why this is a big mistake is that with a seminar or workshop, people can see your body movements and facial expressions and it is much easier to create audience engagement in those situations.

Prior to television being invented, people were used to hearing a radio and the people delivering the radio program sat or stood behind microphones and talked or sang.

When television first came along, guess what presenters did? They sat or stood behind microphones and talked or sang. That's right: they failed to capitalize on the extra dimension of sight that was now available to the audience. With webinars, it's exactly the opposite: you lose a dimension and it's therefore a little trickier to create the audience engagement you enjoy at a physical event, especially when your attendees have access to email and all sorts of other distractions on their computer. Therefore, that missing dimension must be compensated for in order to gain the same level of engagement that's possible in a seminar or workshop.

That said, let's look at why webinars tick the boxes of all 10 ideal Marketing Medium characteristics. Done right, they produce very high-quality leads and they can be run for as little as $100 a month (with some platforms, even less).

Webinars are also quite simple and easy to run (more on that in a moment), are highly scalable, can reach a global audience and once practised will feel completely natural.

Once you have created an effective marketing webinar, you can then automate them, drive traffic to them, and generate leads while you're asleep or on holiday, quite literally.

And given the relatively small budget that you need to run a webinar, they deliver an exceptionally high ROI and can be "rinse and repeated" time and again to different audiences using my OPN strategy (see later in this chapter).

I'm aware that there may be some readers who freak out because webinars are technology-based (a colleague of mine refers to such a person most unkindly as an "e-tard"). So if you fall into that category, then I would urge you to refrain from freaking out before you answer the following questions.

Can you drive a car?

If you answered yes, then there is no doubt in my mind whatsoever that you can, with a little training, drive a webinar and generate leads from it.

Even my most technologically challenged clients, having undertaken my training, grow to love the efficiency and effectiveness of generating leads through webinars.

Here's another slide from one of my presentations on the subject of generating leads through webinars:

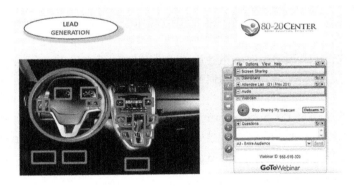

The image on the left shows the dashboard of a car and the image on the right shows the dashboard of the webinar. If you think of all of the things that you do without thinking when driving a car in order to get from A to B safely, there's a heck of a lot going on.

You're accelerating with one foot, breaking with another, steering with your hands, using indicators, changing radio stations, adjusting the air-conditioning, reading the dashboard and potentially a whole lot more. All this while probably thinking about something else.

Contrast those options to your options on the webinar dashboard and I think you'll agree that with a little training even the most technologically challenged "e-tard" can be up and running with webinars in a matter of weeks.

One benefit of running webinars that I should briefly touch on is this: when I exited my last business, I did so almost simultaneously with falling in love with the woman who is now my wife.

This brought about a "tree change" because we started to live together in a small town located in the hinterland. So I went from running seminars and workshops in conference centres across multiple cities and countries to living in a relatively isolated area.

And because I had just exited my previous business, I had some time on my hands to sit down and think about what I was doing next.

I decided that I'd had enough of commuting and flying and so I looked for a business that I could get up and running from the peaceful sanctuary which was our new home.

As synchronicity would have it, that was 2008 which is when Citrix launched "Go To Webinar". I immediately signed up and was one of the early adopters of using webinars to not only generate leads, but to also deliver value.

Today I live in a place widely regarded as heaven on earth. I walk out the back gate of our house through hundred meters of parkland and down a few steps onto the beach.

My daily commute is spent traversing the 10 meters between the espresso machine in our kitchen and my home office. Furthermore, because my wife is German and holds a European passport, we could just as easily operate my business in Europe or the United Kingdom should we choose to do so.

Using webinars to generate leads and deliver value opens up a whole new vista of lifestyle and wealth-generation opportunities.

Also, attendees of webinars demonstrate many attributes that make for a great client: the ability to turn up, the ability to persist (through to the end of the webinar), the desire to be informed, respect for a credible authority, and thoughtful rather than reactive decision-making.

It's a big mistake to make your content/Marketing Message too easily consumable by prospects because it tends to attract more lazy and naive prospects as opposed to when they need to sit still for an hour in order to consume your content/Marketing Message.

Consider this also: when an advertisement comes on the radio or TV, most people will reach for the mute button or go on to something else until the advertisement is over. However, with a highly engaging webinar, they are actually sitting through an extended version of your Marketing Message. If you are engaging enough, then they are carefully paying attention to every word.

This special ability of webinars to attract these higher-quality prospects is also evident in the next Marketing Leg.

MARKETING LEG #2: IN-PERSON SEMINARS AND WORKSHOPS

My second favourite Lead Generation Marketing Medium are seminars and workshops.

They are still scalable in that you're working "one to many" and again, done right, are tremendously effectively generators — in fact they are more effective generators than webinars. It's just that they are not as efficient and they are also a lot more trouble to organise and more expensive to run.

But, if you know how to get bums on seats, then there is no question that running live, face-to-face, seminars and workshops is without peer in respect to generating high-quality, inbound new client enquiries.

Just so there is no confusion, I'll restate why webinars are still my number one favourite for Lead Generation: while face-to-face seminar/workshops are more effective generators, webinars are more cost effective (by a long shot) and therefore offer a much higher return on investment, while at the same time being globally scalable as well as potentially automated.

The trick to generating inbound leads from running your own seminar/workshops is the use of a feedback form at the end of the event with an offer on it for an initial Consult of some description, or a similar follow-up request.

The feedback form must be physically handed to attendees and needs to include the opportunity for them to rate your presentation as well as an offer mentioned above. The critical mistake that most people make in this process is asking attendees to hand in their feedback prior to leaving at some point, and thereby failing to remain in control of the feedback form process.

You must stay in control of the process of completing the feedback forms *and* having them handed back in. This can be achieved by offering a prize draw for your book or something else, which will induce people to fill out the feedback form. In my experience, people to love the idea of winning something, so it might even work for simply offered chocolate fish!

So you should inform everyone that they need to complete the feedback form in order to be in the prize draw, and that it's fine if they only put their name on the top and hand that in. The reason for giving them those instructions is simple: you find that once people start writing their name, many continue on to complete the rest of the form. You just have to get them to start writing.

You then have the forms collected and pick someone from the audience to draw one out. You give the winner your prize and ask everyone to applaud their success and in one fell swoop you have just collected a whole bunch of fresh, high-quality, inbound leads.

A question I get quite often from Advisors is whether they should do webinars or seminar/workshops. My answer is to do both. One-legged stools have a habit of falling over and even three leg stools fall over exponentially more often than four-legged stools.

In addition to running your own seminar/workshops as a lead generator, getting booked as a professional speaker is also a tremendously effective strategy for generating high-quality, in-bound new client enquiries.

MARKETING LEG #3: A *PHYSICAL* BOOK

Recommended Marketing Medium number three is to write a book and publish it physically.

Why a high-quality book is a high-quality Marketing Medium

In light of my first three recommendations which are to run webinars, run seminar/workshops and to write a book, you've probably noticed that I favour those Marketing Mediums that require people to invest time. This singles them out as open-minded, growth-orientated, willing to seek out respected authority figures, displaying a significant degree of intelligence, and willing to invest time, if not money.

What most marketers fail to understand is that the more time a prospect invests in exploring both your content/Marketing Message and/or sales information, the more likely it is that they will buy from you rather than someone else, and be less price-sensitive.

The other critically important benefit of pushing your Marketing Message through mediums that require a prospect to commit a degree of time and also requires them to persist (attending a webinar or viewing the replay, going to the time and trouble of attending your seminar/workshop, going to the trouble of ordering a book and at the very least partially consuming some of the content) is that those people who do so are infinitely more likely to complete the full length of whatever program, course or engagement period you offer.

To be clear: it should not be enough to satisfy you that someone has simply paid you money to work with you. For a whole bunch of reasons, not least of which have to do with karma and filling your Life Purpose and sleeping well at night, you need to get people to consume your Value Delivery and implement your recommendations. Otherwise they are not going to receive any benefit from what you do and you will not have changed the world one iota and they will not be referring anyone to you.

For you to achieve fulfilment of your Life Purpose and for you to receive referrals from your clients, they have to gain value and they don't gain value unless they consume and implement your recommendations. Therefore we want to attract people who are more likely to persist through the entire consumption of your program/course/engagement as well as implementing, and someone who invests the time to consume your Marketing Message contained in the webinar/seminar/workshop/book is exponentially more likely to do the same when they choose to work with you.

The length of your book

Before I delve into what your book should contain, I'll answer one commonly asked question, which is how long a book should be. My advice is the book should be as long as it takes to get the job done and then as short as possible, with one caveat.

I'll explain.

In Leadsology®, webinars, seminars/workshops and books all have similar objectives, the ultimate objective being to generate high-quality, inbound new client enquiries.

Breaking that objective down into a series of sub goals looks something like this:

1. To establish yourself as an expert

2. To establish the idea that you can relate to your audience's current situation (I call this establishing relatability)

3. To establish believability by demonstrating that you know exactly what they have tried previously and informing them of why it didn't work

4. To reveal to your audience what their life will be like after they have implemented your advice

5. To ensure that your audience understands that attempting to implement your advice on their own without specialist help (yours) would be folly

6. To act as an asset/key that unlocks the doors to Other Peoples' Networks (more on this later in the section on OPN)

By way of example, take a look at the structure of this book and see where I tick the first five of the above boxes.

The very fact that I am a *published author* together with my short *biography* on the back cover of this book, together with the quite extraordinary *client results* outlined in the last part of this book are more than sufficient to establish myself as a credible expert with all but the most sceptical and cynical of people, whom I would not want as clients anyway.

In Part One of this book I revealed the "before" picture of your life prior to implementing my recommendations and I also revealed the "after" picture of what your life would look like once you are In Demand.

In Part Two, I established both *relatability* and *believability* by outlining a whole bunch of things that you've tried that didn't work, and I explained to you why they didn't work. I'm pretty confident that you are able to relate to at least several of these mistakes.

The beautiful thing about this particular book is that you gain value on two levels.

The first level is the same as any other well-written book in that you will gain valuable insights and information in regard to its subject matter.

The second level is that now that I've revealed my reasons for the structure and content of this book, you gain further value because I've pulled back the curtain on those reasons and on my motivations.

I do this, of course, in the interests of giving you, my valued reader, as much value as possible, thereby encouraging you to engage in our online community at **www.facebook.com/groups/leadsology/**

So that gives you an excellent overview on how to structure your book, webinar, and seminars/workshops.

Warning: Avoid the SLB

I mentioned that your book should be long enough to get the (above) job done and then as short as possible.

However, I also mentioned one caveat and that is that you must avoid producing an SLB.

I'm going to apologise at this point for swearing, but I feel compelled to do so in order to underline what I consider to be a grave mistake made by many self-published authors.

Over the last several years, there's been a rise in the number of SLB's out there. The initials SLB stand for Shabby Little Book which is a label I use to describe books of less than 40,000 words.

The latter is the widely accepted minimum length that a publisher would accept. I have no idea what the publisher's reasons are for this, but I do know what my reasons are for refusing to put a book out into the marketplace with my name on it with even one word less than 40,000. Here's why...

If I can put my name on the cover of the book, then I want the thing to not only be impressive but to look impressive.

We explored the concept of the Book Cover earlier and how important it was for that Book Cover to reflect the quality of what was inside - this being a metaphor for the value/service that you deliver.

Getting back to the actual book, as opposed to the metaphor: a book's cover is measured by its width, length, and depth. If that's unimpressive, then it suggests equally unimpressive content.

As an extension of that reason, consider also the implications of a lot of books being purchased online these days.

Because the books are being marketed online, the actual size of the book is difficult to ascertain, especially with super-enhanced 3D graphic images.

The last thing I want is for someone to see my book online, to get (hopefully) mildly excited about its content and then to receive the physical book only to find it so thin you could slide it under a door.

Regardless of the quality of the content, the law of first impressions applies in that, if the book size is underwhelming, then it will automatically trigger an unconscious association that the content will be similarly disappointing.

In summary, in publishing an SLB, an author risks being perceived as both unimpressive and underwhelming, thereby creating a result that is completely and totally the opposite of the result we were setting out to achieve — to establish massive credibility, believability and relatability.

Books can be used in so many different ways and I will outline a few of the best ones right here.

Why your book should be in a physical format

A lot of people make the mistake of publishing an e-book and doing only that.

The first reason why physical books are so much better is that they don't drop off the radar scope of the mind quite as quickly or easily. Think about the last time you downloaded an e-book. Did you read it? You know where it is sitting right now? Or did it get buried amongst hundreds of other digital files and is now completely lost somewhere on your computer? Probably even worse, you may not even remember what it was about.

Contrast that to a physical book that sits on someone's desk or coffee table potentially for weeks and months. That's *your* Marketing Message on the cover of the book, it's your name on the cover of the book and that means *you've* got "share of mind" in your prospect's life for a significant period of time.

The second reason deals with credibility and competitive advantage.

Virtually anyone can pump out any book quickly and cheaply. Heck, there are even people online who will write one for you literally for five dollars!

With the barriers to entry for e-books set so low, it means there are an awful lot of e-book authors out there. But there are, relatively speaking, very few authors of physically published books out there.

I've been fortunate to have my writings published in 27 countries and this was before the advent of e-books. That gives me a massive credibility edge over anyone who simply publishes an e-book.

Another caveat

A very low percentage of books, e-books or physical books actually get read in their entirety. Just yesterday a publisher told me that it was estimated that for every 10 books that are purchased, seven are only partially read or never even get opened.

That said, you may be wondering why I'm still hot and frothy about getting you to write a book.

The reason is that even though much of your book won't get read, your Marketing Message, embedded in the title of your book, and your name on the cover of the book, and your biography on the back of the book, will likely get read and frankly that's enough for the book to have done its job for the type of person who is not going to read the whole book. For the others who do actually read either a significant portion, or all of your book, it will be even more effective.

How to use your book to generate leads

You book is essentially a brochure/business card/advertisement all rolled into one. It can be sent to a potential client or Joint Venture partner ahead of meetings, or indeed after a meeting in order to further enhance your credibility. It also can invoke the law of psychological reciprocity (more on that in the section on OPN below) thereby increasing the likelihood that the recipient will work with you rather than someone else.

Given that your book is a brochure/business card/advertisement all rolled into one, it should contain a call to action/and offer.

Typically I recommend to a client that they nominate a website address on the back cover so the traffic can be driven to a specific landing page where an offer can be articulated in more detail than can be accommodated on the back cover of the book. Some clients choose to offer an initial consult to see if the reader's needs fit with their skill set.

Others choose to directly promote a program or course or series of free training videos and so on. By nominating a specific landing page, you can easily change the offer if you choose to do so. Whereas if you have all the details of the offer in the book and you then want to change the offer at a later point in time, you've got to have the book reprinted. And trust me, you *will* change the offer at some point.

Another great idea for generating leads is to include a bookmark with the book on which you promote your offer and the benefits of the offer. It's a whole lot easier to print a new bookmark if you change the offer than it is to change the book.

It's quite important to remember that your book is not just an ordinary book and that's because it includes an offer/call to action and, therefore, anyone who buys it potentially is someone who will make an enquiry.

Books can be offered to the registrants of your webinars and seminars/workshops, which is another way to generate even more leads from these events.

And you can also create exclusive offers so that anyone you know who has a network of your Ideal Clients can be seen to be doing the members of that network a huge favour by arranging to make your book available for free with buyers only paying for a modest postage/packaging/handling fee. That ensures an automatic increase in the quality of the leads which are generated from the book. This effectively means that the marketing of your services is being joyfully undertaken by others.

Your book can also generate leads from Pay-Per-Click advertising such as what is offered by Facebook and Google.

You also generate leads from your book through clients and other purchasers who recommend or give a copy of your book to their friends and/or colleagues.

And if you are targeting CEOs, then you know how hard it is to get in front of them. Sending a professionally produced book with a well-written cover letter is one of the very best ways to get a CEO's attention. Suddenly, in the mind of your prospect, you no longer are just another salesperson with a pitch to deliver. You are an author and a specialist in your particular subject.

Another way of generating leads from the book is by publishing press releases at the time of launch. There are any number of excellent public relation Advisors who can help you to do this.

In the previous section, I wrote about how to generate leads from seminar/workshops that you put together yourself, and how to generate leads from professional speaking engagements. I also mentioned that you can promote your book, including the offer that's included in it, at these events. But the beautiful thing about this particular marketing leg is it works both ways: a book will also get you speaking gigs and becomes a virtuous cycle...the book gets you the gigs and the gigs sell the book...rinse and repeat. Now that's a beautiful thing.

Self-publishing versus being published

I'd recommend that you self-publish your book unless a publisher gives you full and unconditional rights to reprint the book, and to promote personally as opposed to purely through the publishers outlets. The reason for this is that the primary purpose of the book is not to generate direct cash flow, but rather to generate high-quality, inbound new client enquiries which will in turn generate far more cash flow than 99 percent of authors could ever hope for through the payment of any royalties.

The first book that I wrote was picked up by a North American publishing house and I was so overjoyed to be a published author that I didn't really care about the level of royalties. It was just as well, because the amount of royalties relative to the number of books sold was nothing short of pathetic. Fortunately I had followed my own advice and gained permission from the publisher to continue self-publishing and self-promoting the book, and I generated far more revenue from speaking engagements and new clients than the royalties could ever have delivered.

In summary, because the purpose of the book is Lead Generation, be prepared to give the book away for free so long as people are prepared to pay a modest amount for postage/handling/packaging.

Don't feel that you have to make a profit from selling the book. If you can break even, then that's ideal, and this is what we call a self-liquidating offer. The offer pays for itself so your costs are covered but you generate leads.

I found that if you can get a high quality but lower cost printer, and you charge $10 postage/packaging/handling, then you set the bar just about right to cover your costs. This charge will make it more likely that you will attract buyers who are a benefit for your services than if you simply offered the book for free with no charge for postage/packaging/handling.

Ironically, the worst way to generate revenue from your book is by selling it.

The Interplay between the four legs of your marketing stool

I've already mentioned the fact that a book can generate speaking gigs and the speaking gigs can generate book sales — I referred to that as a virtuous cycle.

The same applies to webinars, but in a slightly different way. Note that I don't normally mention the fact that I have written a book during webinars. That's because I'm normally promoting something else — either an initial consult or course/program — and I don't want people mistakenly believing that if they purchase the book then they can get the inside scoop and go ahead and implement on their own. Instead, I'll make my normal offer (initial consult or course/program) and bank the results from that offer, then wait two weeks before we offer the book to those who registered.

Note that any offer you make during a webinar or seminar/workshop should come *after* you presented content that's incredibly engaging and valuable. I feel compelled (as you should too) to deliver high-quality, valuable content in order to earn the right to make an offer. As the old Scottish Presbyterian Minister advised his junior apprentice who had just delivered a fire-and-brimstone sermon "sonny, if you canna feed the sheep, dinna shear them".

Marketing Leg #4: Social Media

You will discover in the next chapter that I have a high standard for my clients in that I ask them to commit to one direct response marketing campaign each week. That means that there is an occasion or event each week where multiple numbers of prospects are being asked to respond to a call-to-action.

You'll also note that each of the first three marketing legs contained an offer/call-to-action of some description.

The fourth Marketing Medium has no call-to-action or offer because its purpose is simply to keep your Brand in their Brain until they are ready to Buy (refer to The Drip Tray and The Three D's of Marketing mentioned in Part Two of this book).

This is where Social Media including Facebook, Twitter, LinkedIn, Instagram, Pinterest, podcasting, blogging and any others amongst the plethora of available platforms may be relevant to your target market.

When I publish a blog or anything similar such as a video blog interview, then our online email platform (www.iContact.com) allows us to post it to our business Facebook page, to Tweet it and post it to our nominated LinkedIn group, with the click of just a few buttons. And most other online email platforms will allow you to do the same.

This is fantastic because it means you get to repurpose your content across multiple platforms. But remember the purpose of these mediums is to simply keep the Brand in the Brain until they are ready to Buy. Those following your tweets or following your Facebook posts will be able to access your content. And provided you offer valuable content, many followers will pay attention when you publish the subject and date of your next webinar or seminar/workshop, or indeed when your new book is launched.

Bonus Marketing Leg: Online Funnel

There is a LOT of buzz around the power of Pay-Per-Click advertising, the primary sources being Facebook adverts (arguably the best online lead source currently available), Google Ad Words and banner advertisements on various websites.

There is no doubt in my mind whatsoever that online marketing should be a part of most Advisors' marketing mix. The brevity of this particular part should in no way convey any form of aversion to generating leads using the above mediums, despite the fact that the overall quality of lead is going to be lower because of their "cold" nature.

My cautionary caveat is simply that source matters. If you can generate hot (ex-clients, word-of-mouth referrals, other referrals) and warm (read your book, attended your webinar/talk) leads, then I would start with those Marketing Mediums, get some runs on the board, cash in the bank, and then turn your marketing guns to the world of online funnels.

Other Peoples' Networks (OPN)

I've generated millions of dollars in revenue for myself and my clients since I discovered the concept of OPN in 1995.

I've developed specific proprietary strategies that will open the door and allow me and my clients to ethically push their Marketing Messages into Other Peoples Networks in a content/value-rich manner.

What follows are the critically important key principles that demonstrate what you need to get right in order to open the door to Other Peoples Networks.

Running webinars and seminars/workshops are all very well and good, but where are you going to draw the attendees from?

Even if you have a large and hungry list of subscribers, they will become less and less responsive if they are simply hearing from you all the time with the same Marketing Message.

By contrast, OPN gives you an inexhaustible flow of new subscribers, new prospects, new attendees and ultimately new clients.

OPN is the fastest way to grow a list and it, metaphorically speaking, is the seat on a four-legged stool that holds the legs together because it feeds each of those legs fresh prospects/followers.

There are four steps to developing your OPN network. An OPN network is a network of people who are prepared to push *your* Marketing Message by way of webinar, seminar/workshop, and your book; into their network.

OPN Step One: ID your target

You're looking for the head of a network with the same Ideal Client as you, or a person of influence in your target market.

Another important characteristic of these people is that they don't perceive you as a threat because they are offering a complimentary service to the same target market, or they are offering a similar service but are mature enough to understand that it's a very large market and some people on their list will never buy from them, but will buy from you and vice versa.

The final and critical characteristic of these people is that they are a good self-promoter (if you target executives in the corporate market), which you can tell from their LinkedIn profile and general web presence, or they are actively marketing (if they are in the business-owner market).

OPN Step Two: Invoke the Law of Psychological Reciprocity

I know that sounds like a heck of a mouthful so let me explain.

In 1964, a very clever psychologist by the name of Eric Berne published a book called *Games People Play*. The book did okay. In fact the book is still available today some 50 years later and so far it's sold over 5 million copies. So it's fair to say that a few people thought it contained an important message.

Dr. Berne used the word "strokes" to describe interactions between people. For example, if I say *"hello"* to Sam then I've given him one stroke. But if I say *"hello, Sam"* then I've given him two strokes. And if I give Sam two strokes, then he will feel compelled to give me two strokes back and possibly even to add a third by adding *"how are you"*. In which case, I will feel obligated to give Sam the third stroke back by responding by saying "I'm well thanks, and how are you?" .

Back in the 1960s, this was called Transactional Analysis and at the risk of doing the great Doctor a grave disservice, I would simply say that we like to keep the score even.

For example, if we get invited for dinner to a friend's home, we will take wine and possibly flowers because we like to keep the score even; and even though the host has insisted that we bring nothing, we just simply don't feel comfortable with that.

In summary, when you do something totally cool for someone else without any (overtly obvious) strings attached, they will want to keep the score even. This does *not* mean they will necessarily agree to whatever proposal you follow up with. But if you've selected your target right and the proposal is beneficial to them, then it's a lot more likely they will say yes to what you suggest if you've done something cool for them first.

Another way of saying this is that you are creating not only a relationship of know, like and trust, but also a measure of unconscious indebtedness.

Here are a few examples of how some people invoke the law of psychological reciprocity.

- Repost someone's blog
- Retweet someone's Tweet
- Publish someone's article
- Invite them to present to your network

Remember, it's very important that you practice going into these transactions with zero expectation, even though it will be hard to get it out of the back of your mind that you want something in return for the cool thing you're doing for this person. You'll get better at this if you simply create a "no strings attached" intention by repeating an affirmation such as *"I clear my mind of all expectation in this venture"*. As you practice with this sort of affirmation, you will slowly reprogram your mind to the point where you just do a bunch of cool things to key people of influence, and build a network of such people with whom you have a relationship of know, like and trust.

The Pick Up Test

One question I receive quite often is about how to tell when you've established a relationship of know, like and trust. That's a great question because we need some form of litmus test to know the right time to approach your key person with a Joint Venture proposal, or cross-marketing proposal, or whatever value exchange you have in mind.

I can answer this question with another question: if you called this person's mobile phone and your name appeared on their phone, would they happily take the call? If so, then you've established a relationship of know, like and trust and you can proceed with your proposal.

OPN Step Three: Use the Prius Factor to create even more "know, like and trust"

Japanese car manufacturers Honda and Toyota launched their new hybrid vehicle models at approximately the same time. As you probably know, a hybrid vehicle has two sources of power, a standard fossil-fuel-burning petrol engine and electricity. When the electricity is not powerful enough to propel the car forward at an acceptable speed, then the petrol engine kicks in and it recharges the battery in the car as it runs. So it's a more environmentally friendly vehicle.

What happened after the worldwide launch in 2000 puzzled marketers for quite some time. Although both vehicles were similarly priced with similar specifications and were produced by manufacturers with brands that represented similar quality, the Toyota Prius went on to outsell the Honda equivalent by a ratio something like 7 to 1.

After some research, the reason for Toyota's phenomenal success became clear. When Honda launched its hybrid, it simply took the chassis/body of its bestselling Honda Civic, put in a hybrid engine and a small badge on the boot/trunk of the car next to the word "Civic". Toyota, on the other hand, created a whole new vehicle shape, which some would say was ugly but which was undeniably a totally different shape from literally every other vehicle on the road. And so it stood out and was instantly recognised by anyone who knew anything about this new and exciting concept called hybrid cars.

The reason why Toyota slaughtered Honda in the sale of hybrids became clear: even more than wanting to be environmentally friendly, the owners of the Toyota Prius wanted to be *seen* to be environmentally friendly, and the distinctive shape of the Prius achieved that. Honda finally woke up to the research, but not until 2013 when the Honda Fit was launched with a distinctive new shape. They soon began to beat Toyota for market share in the hybrid car sector.

The morale of The Pius Factor story is this: you can build on the power of Psychological Reciprocity by adding yet another layer of know, like and trust that is achieved when you make your key person of influence look amazingly good in front of their network.

OPN Step Four: The Godfather Strategy

There is a scene in the 1972 movie The Godfather where the character Johnny Fontaine is trying to buy is way out of a singing contract. He asks the head of a major mafia crime family, Vito Corleone, his Godfather, for help in persuading the bandleader to sign an agreement allowing him to be released from the contract. Fontaine complains to the Godfather who responds with the immortal words *"we are just going to have to make him an offer he can't refuse"*.

The mafia boss orders his personal assassin to place a gun to the bandleader's forehead and tell him that either his signature would be on the agreement or his brains. That's certainly what I'd call an offer that is hard to turn down!

Now at the risk of stating the bleeding obvious, I am *not* suggesting that you buy yourself a gun and start waving it in the face of a key person of influence. What I am suggesting is that, once you have invoked the Law of Psychological Reciprocity and The Prius Factor, you then get creative in coming up with a win-win proposal for potential Joint Venture or cross marketing opportunities. Possibilities include, but are not limited to, some form of exposure to each other's networks, be that releasing an interview of each other to each network, or reciprocal presentations to each other's networks, or some form of direct response offer to each other's networks.

CHAPTER #5:
THE MODEL

GETTING YOUR BUSINESS Model right is critically important to ensure that your capacity to scale Value Delivery, and thereby help more people and make more money in less time, is maximised.

The term "Business Model" refers to a big picture view of your business and will answer more of the Strategic Questions that we covered earlier in this book. Additional questions will include the range of services that you offer and how you lead people from one service to another.

(BTW: the reason why a business *plan* is almost always worse than useless for Advisors and other small business owners is well-documented in my previous book, *The Million-Dollar Ceiling* which can be purchased from **www.million-dollarceiling.com/book/** Note that in that book I also outline an alternative to the traditional business plan.)

By way of example, let's have a look at the traditional coaching model and see how we can re-engineer the Business Model to dramatically scale revenue and Value Delivery, and how to achieve that with a lot less time. If you are a consultant or a trainer or CPA/accountant or anyone else offering advice or a service then you can apply the exact same principles to transform your business model from one that generates relatively low revenue, but demands high hours, to exactly the opposite.

Most business coaches have one offering that is usually a 12-month coaching engagement whereby they meet with the client perhaps twice a month to create and implement a business plan. The client pays a set monthly fee, but approximately 87 percent of such engagements fail to endure beyond the six-month mark, occasionally because the business coach is not delivering results, but more often because the client is not implementing.

This traditional business model for business coaches is a recipe for stress and very often a business coach who operates this way suffers from the classic Roller Coaster symptoms mentioned earlier in Part One, whereby at the top of the rollercoaster there is plenty of client work but no time to enjoy the cash generated, and at the bottom of the rollercoaster there is plenty of time but not enough client work to generate cash to enjoy it.

Many of my consultant, coaching and training clients have come on board because they liked the sound of re-engineering the business model into what I call "Front End" and "Back End" services. Some of these can be quite elaborate, but below I'll illustrate the principle with a simple version.

Firstly though, let's have a look at some of the questions that I like to sign off on prior to giving a new client the green light on their new Business Model.

1. What is the "wow" that I will deliver?

2. Who will I deliver it to?

3. How can I reach them? (we answered this in the previous chapter)

4. How fast can I get into "wow"?

5. In what format do I want to deliver the value?

6. How will I segment my Value Delivery into Front End and Back End

7. How much money will they pay for it? (I call this "Doing The Maths")

8. How much time will it take me to deliver it? (I call this "Doing The Time")

9. How many leads do I need to generate in order to hit my revenue targets?

Once these questions are answered effectively, we've then got a shot at generating more than $1 million of revenue per year in roughly 3 to 5 days per week, depending on what stage of implementing the model you're at (more time is needed at the start and less time is needed once you're up and running).

It's always surprised me how few owners of business start-ups actually sit down to "Do The Maths" and "Do The Time". For example, a mobile dog washing service can probably handle five dogs a day for five days a week at $80 a dog. That adds up to $2,000 a week, minus business operating expenses including vehicle, depreciation, shampoos and so on. That means the operator is going to take home around about $1,000 a week on which he/she will have to pay tax. So let's say they net $700 a week, which means they are batting at $17.50 an hour. Which sucks.

Fortunately, most Advisors make a whole lot more than that, but nevertheless they are often still severely limited in generating more significant revenue flows simply because they are operating primarily on the "time equals money" formula.

Having established that, let's look at a simple way to re-engineer the traditional business coaching model.

There are a whole bunch of problems/opportunities/challenges that the vast majority of a business coaches' clients will have. For example, how to use their time more productively, how to recruit top performers, how to set each of the team members up with clear goals, how to develop the team members and keep them inspired and motivated and focused, how to get new clients in the door, how to develop and run quality control systems, and a whole lot more.

Once you've identified the problem/opportunity/challenges that are common to the vast majority of your target market, then you find common, generic solutions and create training, templates, guides, checklists and action assignments for each one of those problem/opportunity/challenges.

You break each of these issues down into a series of small steps and you record webinars which, once they've been perfected, can be consumed by a group of clients simultaneously while you are on holiday or asleep.

And instead of trying to sign up a client for 12 months, you give them an eight-week value proposition. The reason you do this is that's a much easier duration of value proposition to market, especially when you guarantee your program, which you most certainly should in some form or another.

By running a group program, you automatically scale your revenue dramatically, and by pre-recording the Value Delivery/training, you equally dramatically decrease the amount of time required of you to deliver value.

The trick here is to still charge a premium price for your service. Remember that clients don't care how you deliver the value so long as you deliver. Sure, there will be the odd person who doesn't want to be part of the group program. There's a simple answer you can give them when they ask if they can work with you one-on-one. Just tell them that if they want to work with you one-on-one, all they need to do is add a zero onto the end of the price of your group program and then you'll work with them one on one.

So let's say we put 12 clients into your program — and please note that I've had as many as 140 on the same program at the same time, so I think the number 12 is more than realistic.

Once a week they sit down and do the training on their computer and download their action assignment and complete it using the templates, guides, transcripts, checklists et cetera that you provide.

When they complete their assignment, they upload it to a closed Facebook group where others can view their results and learn from their work and vice versa. You receive a notification when someone posts to the group and you put aside an hour each day over four days a week to review their assignments. You also host a live Coaching Q&A webinar once a week to answer the questions.

You offer graduates of this Front End/Initial Program a Back End/ Graduate program that runs for 12 months.

Here's what Doing The Maths looks like for this new model:

INITIAL PROGRAM

- 12 clients / program @ $7,500 each = $90,000 / program
- Each program runs for 2 months
- 5 programs per year = 60 clients
- Subtotal $450,000 revenue per year (average $37,500 per month)

GRADUATE PROGRAM

- 25 percent of graduates = 15 graduate clients @ $25,000 each
- Program runs for 12 months
- 1 program per year
- Subtotal = $375,000 per year (average $31,250 per month)

Total after 12 months = $450,000 + $375,000 = $825,000

This is an average of $68,750 per month

Now let's have a look at what Doing The Time looks like:

Running this model would generate $68,750 per month for working no more than an average of two days a week absolute maximum, including all preparation and delivery time (remember however you still need to develop the actual content). Add on to that a week for marketing your program and you've got three days a week or 24 hours a week, which adds up to 960 hours over a 40-week year or $859.73 per hour. I think you'll agree that's a little better than the $80 an hour most business coaches earn using the traditional model.

Is it possible?

Absolutely!

I've done it and I'm doing it again, plus I know of others who are earning many tens of thousands every month with this model and some who are generating well over $100,000 a month.

As mentioned before, there are many variations on this Front End/ Back End style model. With an open mind and a bit of creativity, it's simply quite extraordinary the transformation that you can witness when you commit to developing a Business Model along the lines that I've just outlined.

CHAPTER #6:
THE MARKETING

GIVEN THE PLETHORA of different ways we can get a message into the market, especially in these days of diversified Social Media platforms, it's not surprising that I'm sometimes asked what the most important thing is in respect to being successful at marketing.

My answer is *"do some"*. People often smile at this, but it's very true; even marketing done poorly is better than no marketing activity at all.

Having said that, we can get a whole lot more sophisticated than that in terms of setting up a structure for your marketing that will produce a lot of high-quality, inbound new client enquiries.

This chapter looks at a series of concepts and strategies that will seriously turbocharge your Lead Generation success. They are the product of 35 years of sales, marketing and management experience. I would therefore encourage you to study them well.

THE GOLD STANDARD

I ask my clients to really step up in terms of their commitment to marketing. I've already mentioned the Poland Weekly Calendar system, in which every Wednesday is devoted to nothing else but marketing.

Included on that Wednesday is one direct response marketing event/campaign whereby clients are asked to buy something from you, perhaps in the form of ordering a book, or paying for initial pre-client-engagement Consult, or joining your program. Does this event have to be on Wednesday? Absolutely not! So long as it happens once a week I don't really give a hoot exactly when it happens.

But the Wednesday (or whatever other days a week you nominate) is set aside to set up that event/campaign so that the leads and sales are flowing in almost every single week of the year. This is what I call the Gold standard: one direct response marketing event/campaign every week of the year, with the possible exception of the week between Christmas and New Year.

THE THREE D'S OF MARKETING

To be fair, this is not a critical concept but it does answer a question that I often get which is: *"okay, I've bought into the idea of having one Marketing Day every single week, but what the heck am I going to do on that day because I have no idea where to start?"*

Which is a very worthwhile question. And the answer is to think about marketing as having three different categories. There is Marketing Discovery, Marketing Development and Marketing Doing.

To begin with, your Marketing Day is going to be spent reading and doing courses and meeting with your mentor or whatever else you need to do in order to discover what you need to do in respect to your marketing.

Once you've figured out your marketing plan, then your Marketing Day will be spent in the Development of the assets you need in order to execute your marketing. For example, you may decide that you need to write a book, create a webinar/talk/seminar and so on. During this phase, you may actually decide that you need more than one day a week to devote to marketing, and if you can manage that, then you'll certainly accelerate your progress towards the third D, which is where each Marketing Day is spent Doing the marketing.

THE SEGUE

People often struggle with the idea of setting aside one day a week as a Marketing Day.

If that's you, then here's what I suggest: grab your diary/schedule and have a look through *next* month.

Find one day that is clear and free and schedule an appointment for the whole day (yes actually schedule this in your calendar) with yourself and call it "Marketing Day". Then go two months out and find two days in separate weeks and do the same. Repeat this in the third month out, setting aside one day a week for three weeks during that month. I think you'll have figured out by now that I'm then going ask you to go four months out and block out one marketing day per week for each of the four weeks in that month and to do that for each month thereafter.

WhilePeople legitimately tell me that their calendar is so full over the next few weeks they couldn't possibly schedule one whole day for marketing, but I've never had anyone tell me they couldn't perform The Segue as described above.

THE MARKETING CALENDAR

This is not a new concept, but it's a solid one and it follows on from The Gold Standard. You simply grab a calendar and schedule 90 days out a marketing event/campaign covering 13 weeks.

It is possible to schedule further than 13 weeks ahead, but it's a lot harder to keep everything locked in, especially when you're working with joint-venture partners who don't want to commit that far out.

Having identified and scheduled marketing events/campaigns for each week over the next 13 weeks, you then schedule a reminder every single week at the same time to identify the events/campaign for 13 weeks. Because at the end of each week, another week has gone and you need to set something up for what will now be the 13th week.

This way you have a perpetual, rolling, Marketing Calendar which you will definitely *not* stick to 100 percent, but which equally definitely will result in you having conducted a whole lot more marketing events/campaigns then you would have otherwise.

THE FIRST DOMINO

At some stage, you've probably seen some record-breaking attempt at the number of dominoes knocked over by lining thousands of dominoes up and simply flicking the first one to knock over the second and subsequent dominoes.

The First Domino is a concept that I developed over 20 years ago when I was struggling to cope with the complexity of the marketing systems I had developed. It was kind of like being hoisted by my own petard, not that I necessarily know exactly what that means. But you and I probably both understand that it's something about creating a challenge for ourselves.

At the time, I was running group coaching programs for hundreds of entrepreneurs and I needed a lot of high-quality, inbound, new client enquiries to keep my programs full.

I figured out that the concept of Host Beneficiary as outlined by marketing great Jay Abraham was the way to go. Host Beneficiary is where you identify the head of a network that is filled with your Ideal Clients and push your Marketing Message into that network. This is a little different from Joint Ventures because with Host Beneficiary money doesn't change hands.

I identified that CPAs/accountants who worked in the small business market had a virtually endless supply of my Ideal Clients. I also figured out that around 5 percent of them would be open to the idea of me presenting a business-building seminar for their clients. Now 5 percent may not sound like a lot, but trust me it's more than sufficient.

I had done the maths on how many leads I needed and I knew that if I ran one such seminar every week (The Gold Standard) then I get the clients I want.

But there was quite a lot to the whole process of identifying potential hosts, engaging with them, convincing them that this was a great idea, and then actually performing the event.

So I sat down and identified the various segments involved in the whole process and then wrote out a series of checklists which drill down by identifying each individual step that had to take place.

With a relatively complex array of steps/systems before me, I was in danger of being overwhelmed. So I decided I wanted to identify the one thing that, if I did that one thing, would make everything else happen almost automatically.

So my one thing was this: once a month in our boardroom I would host eight CPA/accountants and I would present to them the opportunity of inviting me to present a business-building seminar to their clients.

I had well-trained staff who could handle pretty much everything else after that meeting, using the training and checklists/systems that I provided them.

All I had to do in order to keep the revenue coming in and keep the business growing was get eight CPA/accountants' bums in the seats of my boardroom once a month. That was what I call The First Domino.

These days, I have a different First Domino, but it's exactly the same principle: I have one simple objective every single week that I have to "knock over" and after that everything else falls into place.

So you have to think about your First Domino and then schedule to complete it on your Marketing Day each week.

CHAPTER #7:
THE MEASURES

THERE IS AN immense variety of numbers that you can track for any given business, but for Advisors we can make those numbers very simple without diluting the benefit that comes from tracking.

THE TOP THREE METRICS TO MEASURE

The three top metrics to measure are our revenue, net profit and customer/team satisfaction.

That's enough.

If your revenue is growing and your margins are fat and healthy and your customers/team are really happy, then you've got yourself a great business.

In the book that I referred to previously, *The Million-Dollar Ceiling,* I go into some detail about how to link projects and other events to these three key metrics so that you not only are measuring them, you also are improving them.

That being the case, I won't repeat that information again here, other than to say you would do well to both measure those three metrics each and every month and identify what needs to happen to continually improve them.

MARKETING KPIs TO TRACK

I've seen people present on the subject of Key Performance Indicators, or KPIs as they are known. People in the audience nod sagely in agreement with the presenter while at the same time their eyes glaze over at the breadth and depth of information that the presenter is suggesting they need to track.

As a consequence, they invariably and almost exclusively go back to their respective offices and track nothing.

Instead, I suggest you track some very simple KPIs which will do the job admirably well in terms of keeping you aware of what's actually happening in your business. Those KPIs are as follows:

- Leads generated
- Sales made
- New clients coming on board
- Revenue from existing clients
- Revenue from new clients
- The First Domino (tracking your execution of this becomes a critical KPI)

Set up a weekly meeting with your mentor and another one with your team to make yourself accountable for reviewing all of the above measures. If you're not a numbers person, then have a Virtual Assistant or other Team Member set up a spreadsheet and input the numbers on your behalf.

CHAPTER #8:
YOUR STYLE

YOUR STYLE SIMPLY refers to the idea that whatever marketing and Lead Generation you're engaging in, it needs to fit with your Values (what you hold to be important) and your Vision (what you want your lifestyle and business-style to look like), as well as your personality style.

YOUR VALUES AND VISION

For example, if anyone suggested to you that you should engage in hype or BS-style marketing with the promise of personal financial gain, I'm very confident that you'd feel uncomfortable about that and would decline, without regret. That's a simple example of making sure that your marketing efforts fit your Values.

Equally, if someone showed you a way to make $1 million a year, but that you'd have to work seven days a week and in the process compromise your health, your relationships and your lifestyle, then I'm equally sure you'd decline the offer as well, because it doesn't fit with your Vision of what you want your life to look like.

In regard to your personality style, I often say to new clients that they should let me know if they feel a lot of discomfort with one of my marketing suggestions. Because there's a very good chance that I have 5 or 6 other ways of achieving the same objective using a different method that they would feel fits their personality a lot better.

YOUR ENTREPRENEURIAL DNA

Around 35 years ago, my life changed. One day I was someone else and the next I was me.

The transformation occurred just after I started my first business at age 24. Having always been interested in personal growth, I invested in a multi-perception personality assessment.

To receive my report, I had to find six people who knew me well in a business context and ask them to complete a series of questions in regard to their perceptions of me.

All of the responses were posted to a company in the USA and, six weeks later, a report was received by that firm's local representative. I was then summoned to meet for the debriefing, which involved flying to their office in another city. So it was a bit of a big deal.

What happened next was a shock. So much so that, as I type this 35 years later, I can clearly recall where I was sitting in the room at the time and what I was seeing as my report was displayed on an overhead projector.

I simply didn't recognise the person in the report. *that* person was an ideas-generator, confident and assertive. *he* was a risk-taker, an adventurer and a leader.

I, on the other hand, was careful, unoriginal and a follower of other people's ideas. At least that was my perception, despite having put my first house on the line by starting my own business at such a young age.

As I spoke with the consultant about the report, it slowly dawned on me that my upbringing had created a different "me" from the one I was born to be. In short, I was living a lie. It was a nice lie, but a lie nonetheless. And later that evening when I reflected on the report's findings in my hotel room, I made a decision. I was no longer going to listen to the voices in my head that cautioned me to hold back.

Instead, I chose to back myself. To go with my gut feel. To nurture new ideas and to be more assertive, albeit politely. My life changed almost instantly. More risks, more adventures, more failures and bigger successes.

It was like the report had given me a permission slip to *"be the me I was born to be"*.

The impact was both liberating and motivating at the same time. I no longer followed the business-success rulebook that told me I must do things a certain way. I had discovered a more natural pathway to business and personal fulfilment. The guilt trips and self-doubt faded (never completely, even today) and were largely replaced by increased levels of happiness and fulfilment. As a result, I was more productive and more energised.

And the transition was not hard. It felt like I had just unzipped a full body suit and simply stepped out. It was easy because I was simply relaxing into being me.

Although I couldn't articulate it at the time, the report had identified what I now call my "Entrepreneurial DNA". That's the term I give to the unique combination of natural inclinations and talents that every solopreneur or business owner Advisor possesses.

In 2005 I decided to create a similar system so that solopreneurs and business owners could identify their own Entrepreneurial DNA and thereby benefit as much as I had all those years ago.

In November 2006, after more than a year of testing and refinements, I released the "Entrepreneurial Style Profile," and more recently my team finished creating an online version which is completely free.

Here's the link: **www.collegeforentrepreneurship.com/entrepreneur-profiling-assessment-tool/**

I'm hopeful that in receiving your own personalized Entrepreneurial Style Profile, you'll discover your natural pathway to business wealth and personal fulfilment.

CHAPTER #9: SCALABILITY

I ONCE SAW A documentary on television about the great Henry Ford, the modern day father of the assembly line, and producer of the world-changing Model T Ford.

That inspired me to learn more about the assembly line and how it transformed the entire civilised world in the early part of the twentieth century. If you study the subject in some depth, then I'm confident you'll come to the same conclusion that the previous sentence is not an exaggeration.

It was the principles behind the assembly line that fascinated me, but it was the facts that sparked my fascination.

At one stage, Henry Ford was producing 30 cars per man, per year, while his nearest rival at Packard was producing 2.67 cars per man per year! That's a phenomenal difference.

Not only that, but Ford was paying his workers five dollars a day which was double the average paid by his competitors. In doing so, he destroyed the majority of his competitors and transformed the lifestyle of the average American assembly line worker.

And impressive as all of that is, it doesn't stop there. In addition, Ford was producing higher-quality cars than the vast majority of his competitors, in that they were far more robust and subject to far fewer breakdowns.

When I was reading about this, I became fascinated as to how someone could out-produce his nearest competitor more than 10 times over, pay double the wages of his competitors, produce products of far superior quality, and at the same time be raking in millions of dollars a year more than all of his competitors put together.

What I discovered was the principles behind a vehicle assembly line production could be applied to the delivery of services almost equally well.

Interestingly, the assembly line has been in operation since 1100 A.D. when the Venetians were employing 16,000 workers and producing one ship a day when other shipyards were struggling to produce one every three months.

Also, abattoirs (meat works) have employed assembly-line principles for at least 200 years, and Wedgewood was using an assembly line to produce fine china, porcelain, and luxury accessories as early as 1759.

But it was Henry Ford who took the assembly line to a whole different stratosphere.

When you apply assembly-line principles to the services you offer, your productivity goes up, your revenue goes up, your costs go down, the profit goes up, your effectiveness goes up, your efficiency goes up and so also does the quality of your work.

There are a total of eight assembly-line steps that I work on with my clients but in the interests of giving you something that is simple enough for you to implement and gain value from by reading this book, I'll outline three of them. Those three are Segmentation, Automation, and Delegation.

Assembly-line principles all start with Segmentation, which simply means you break a complex job down into a series of smaller, simpler steps. For example, old Henry figured out that making a Model T Ford involved 7,822 "motions". That was 7,822 movements that workers would have to perform in order to have a Model T rolling of the assembly line.

By way of further example, prior to Ford's assembly-line, vehicle manufacturers (of which there were hundreds in the USA at the time), would have a man specialising in building a dynamo which would produce the electricity required to power the battery that would in turn power the car's headlights and so on.

Ford broke down the manufacturing of a dynamo into a series of small steps, each one being so easy and simple to perform that a man needed a matter of minutes in training in order to be competent at completing that particular step/motion. This resulted in a dynamo being built faster and it also meant that new employees got up to speed with their role super-fast.

Segmentation enables greater productivity and increases quality simultaneously.

❖ ❖ ❖

Segmentation is therefore the first step in integrating assembly-line principles into your business and thereby gaining immense benefits.

Once you've broken down your Value Delivery and your Marketing into a series of small steps, each of which can be systemised (fancy words simply meaning you can create a checklist or guide for each step), then you can figure out which steps can be sent offshore where labour costs are lower, and which steps can be delegated locally. This frees up your time significantly. For more on this concept, refer to Tim Ferris's book *The Four Hour Work Week* .

Once you've Segmented and Delegated, then it's time for Automation. In the physical world, machines can be built to automate manufacturing processes, and very often in the service-based world there are web-based services that perform the equivalent Automation.

By way of a simple example to illustrate Segmentation, Delegation and Automation, consider our joint venture system.

I created checklists and some basic training for a Virtual Assistant to data-mine and identify potential partners. After I've vetted the list, she sends a series of pre-written email templates to each potential partner and tracks responses in a simple tracking spreadsheet.

If our potential partner responds and wants to talk, she provides them with a link to go online and answer some simple questions and then select a time for us to meet using my online scheduler.

Mostly, the first thing that alerts me to the fact that I've got a joint venture under way is that I have an appointment pop-up in my scheduler telling me who I am going to be speaking to, what their target market is, what they offer and other relevant information about the potential for us working together.

Prior to applying the concepts of Segmentation, Delegation and Automation, setting up such a meeting could have literally taken me eight hours or more. Now the whole process is completed with barely 10 minutes of my time each week.

You can apply the principles of Segmentation, Delegation and Automation to every single part your business, including your Value Delivery process and Marketing but also to Human Resource, finances, data tracking, asset development, projects and more.

CHAPTER #10:
STRUCTURE

THE PURPOSE OF this chapter is to show you what it takes to implement the wisdom in this book in your business and thereby transform your lifestyle and business style dramatically.

RAPID IMPLEMENTATION FORMULA

Literally the biggest problem that Advisors complain about in respect to business development and growth is the dreaded F.T.I., or failure to implement.

In 1995, I discovered a formula, taught to me by the great Brian Tracy that pulled back the curtain on how to kill F.T.I. stone dead cold in his tracks.

The formula is this: *time, day, place, person, money*

What that means in simple terms is that you find a Mentor who has a proven track record in showing people how to achieve what it is you want to achieve. You pay them the money they're asking and you commit to meeting with them (in a group or one-on-one) at a particular time and on a particular day and at a particular place every week. Monthly is not frequent enough, because you will drift too much.

There are three types of people who will read this book, as indeed there are three types of people who attend my webinars.

The first type is the person who gained great value from the content, but fails to engage me as a mentor. They tell themselves that they can implement on their own. I've previously addressed why this doesn't work, including the fact that all of this great content will simply fall off the radar scope of the mind as they get distracted and start chasing the next bright shiny thing.

The second type of person is an implementer. They tell themselves pretty much the same thing as the first person, but they do actually implement. I estimate that these people number around 1 percent of my total audience. Unfortunately, they don't implement effectively, because there are so many subtleties that a person can get wrong and the chances of them getting everything right is similar to the chances of a dictionary being the result of an explosion in a printing press.

The third type of person understands the power of *"time, day, place, person, money,"* and they lock themselves into a structure of planning, action, accountability and review.

I invite you to be in the third of the three categories by accepting the offer on the bookmark that came with this book, or by seeing what I've got going on at **www.leadsology.guru**.

And if you'd like to discover the sort of results that others who have worked with me have achieved, then please proceed to Part Four.

❋ ❋ ❋

PART FOUR

RESULTS OF ADOPTING
LEADSOLOGY®

LEADSOLOGY®
RESULTS

THE FOLLOWING ARE comments from clients who have graduated from one of Tom Poland's programs, which are embedded with the principles, strategies and structure of Command+Control.

These results are from clients who "imperfectly persisted" in implementing the strategies from his program. Results like these are not achieved by all clients and results are dependent on many factors external to Tom Poland's control.

 During the first twelve months that I worked with Tom Poland our **revenue increased by 43% to over $1,000,000 and my net personal earning's rose by 50 % to $400,000.**

We achieved the goals with no sacrifice of personal leisure time and we continue to enjoy an "earnings per partner hour" which is amongst the top quartile in the country.

Steve Bennet, Bennet and Associates

Before working with Tom Poland's program I was very clear about where I want to take the business to, but I had no idea of how to get there and I thought, "If I work any harder I'll kill myself."

But while I was working with Tom our turnover exploded, we more than quadrupled our revenue and profits increased by over 300%.

At the same time I worked a lot less. My investment with Tom has paid off more than tenfold. Tom's program certainly delivers on its promises.

Ginny Scott, M.D. Capulet

In the first year of working with Tom my earnings increased by just over 100%.

One of the biggest benefits was discovering how to strengthen my ability to systematically attract very high quality new clients into my practice. In addition I was able to set realistic but challenging goals in my business and personal life to achieve a more realistic work life balance.

Greg Moyle. Managing Director, NZFP

Prior to joining Tom Poland's program I was working 60 – 70 hours a week and I had only one afternoon off work on the weekends. Now a typical work week for me is about three days.

Our profit has tripled and so I'm making a lot more money out of what I'm doing.

Tom's program is priceless. I couldn't put a price on where the program has taken me from and where I am now.

Dianne Bussey, FACT Solutions Consulting

Anything that doubles your income has got to be good and that's exactly what happened while working with Tom Poland.

I gained an additional depth to my personal life and business life.

I've got more leisure time, I have more holidays, and I earn more.

I recommend Tom Poland to anyone in charge of a business.

Geoff Wilson, Professional Consulting Group

Before joining Tom Poland's program around 2000 I was working 60 – 70 hours a week. Once we started working together I grew

my number of employees from six to over 30 and **I sold one of my businesses for many millions thanks in no small part to working with Tom's program.**

I've spent a week with Richard Branson on his private island and dined personally with Google founder Larry Page thanks to Tom challenging me to think bigger and to follow my passion. And I'm pleased to still be working with Tom some eight years later. Joining Tom's program was certainly one of the best business decisions I've ever made.

Mark Rocket, Rocket Lab, Avatar and others

Before working with Tom Poland's program my business was "all me". I was working insane hours and I thought there had to be a better way.

Now I've freed up a lot of time including 12 weeks holiday a year as well as **growing the business by over 400% and adding several million dollars to turnover and the bottom line of my business.**

Fred Soar, Soar Printing

As a result of working with Tom Poland the value of my business increased by many millions of dollars.

Before joining Tom's program I was working six and seven days a week. Now I achieve more and yet I only work four days a week.

My advice for any business owner who wants to enjoy more revenue and a better quality lifestyle, is to get on with it by joining Tom Poland's program.

Grant Faber, Superbrokers Logistics Ltd

In the last 12 months since I started working with Tom Poland my earnings have more than doubled and I'm ahead of my target again this year.

I've gone from having 4 weeks holiday per year to 13 weeks. I've quit smoking, lost 4 kilograms of weight and I'm fitter than I've ever been before. I credit these achievements to my commitment to working with Tom Poland.

If you own a business then it's likely that working with Tom will be the best investment you'll ever make.

Warren Storm, Storm Financial, Life Brokers NZ Ltd

I started working with Tom Poland 18 months ago and already I've doubled my earnings

I now also enjoy three months holidays every year whereas for the last 31 years I've worked almost seven days a week.

I've experienced dramatic changes in both my business and personal life.

John Good, Good Financial Services

Before joining Tom Poland's program I'd reached a point where I couldn't see how I was going to grow the business more because I was drowning in detail.

Now my time is freed up to think more clearly and more creatively. **We've gone from being static to buying out a competitor because we've boosted our profits significantly.**

And time off was always an issue for me but now I take at least one week off every quarter and three weeks at Christmas and I feel good about that. If you are prepared to make changes the value of Tom Poland's program is massive.

Ian Telford, Jason Products

After joining Tom Poland's program **within nine months I've boosted profits and generated more revenue than the last three years put together.**

The actual overall improvement as a complete package in my business has been substantial and that's allowed me to become semi-retired.

Gilbert Chapman, Debt Recovery Group

Prior to working with Tom Poland's program I was running a reasonably successful business but since then **sales have increased and profits have increased quite considerably.**

But the success at work has been balanced by ongoing success at home and with my health as well and that's been important to me.

Tom's programs may appear to be pricey but it's also a question of value because in my case, I've recovered the cost of his program many times over.

Alan Coop, Intercad Ltd

Prior to working with Tom Poland I was working long and hard but the business wasn't growing and I felt frustrated about that.

Thanks to working with Tom my business rapidly increased in value and is now worth millions.

I can think of no reason why anyone who wants to add six or seven figures to their revenue would not apply to join Tom's program.

My investment has paid off a thousand fold. Tom's program worked with me and I know of others who have had a similar result.

Win Charlebois, The Diamond Shop

PART FIVE

NEXT STEPS

NEXT STEPS

LAST NIGHT I watched Roger Federer playing in the Australian Open Tennis Tournament. The "Fed Express" as he's known, holds the record for the number of consecutive weeks at number one in the world (237 weeks) and he's also won a record 17 Grad Slam titles.

If you love tennis then you'd probably agree it would be amazing to hit a tennis ball like Roger.

(And that would be equally true if you're a big admirer of a certain musician or artist or a sports star - it would be pretty awesome to perform at their level.)

But imagine how it would play out, so speak, if Roger Federer wrote a book on how to play tennis including how to serve, play backhand shots, forehand returns, approach shots, overhead smashes and so on.

And imagine also that there's a guy by the name of Sam who wants to learn how to play tennis and so he buys Roger Federer's book, reads it diligently and memorizes every stroke.

And that then, through some minor miracle, Sam's accepted as a wildcard player in one of the four "Grand Slam" tennis tournaments of Australia, USA, France or England.

How do you think Sam would go?

Remember, Sam has read the great Roger Federer's book on how to play tennis. He knows all the theory and he's memorised every technique.

You'll probably agree that unless his opponent double faults, Sam would be in danger of failing to win even one point and he almost certainly won't win a single game, let alone a set or a match.

I'm also pretty sure that you'll agree that the absolute best way for Sam to learn how to play tennis would be to hire Roger Federer to coach him, assuming that Sam could afford to do that, and to have Roger show him how to get the knowledge that's in the book, into his own game.

And it's the same with this book. Knowing the theory is a good start but it's just that, a start. You now need to move forward.

In order to integrate the proven successful Leadsology® Model into your business you *will* need a coach/mental/guide who can teach you exactly how to do that. As mentioned earlier in this book, the reason is simply that there are so many subtleties to get right when it comes to building a Leadsology® Model that's customised for your personality and your service and your marketplace.

And so if you want to work with me here are your options for working with me. Either of these ways will mean that I can "take your hand" and walk with you step by step through process of bringing Leadsology® to life, in your life.

1. You can work with me one on one

I love working with clients one on one but I have limited time available and so I need to be quite selective and you should also know that I'm quite expensive. But if you think that one on one work might be right for you please email **support@leadsology. guru** and we can go from there.

2. You can join my Leadsology® Program

While it's very *unlikely* that Sam could afford to hire Roger Feder-er, it's very *likely* that you'll be able to afford me.

Here's why.

I'm on a mission to change the world, one business at a time. The way I see it, better businesses makes it possible to have a better lives and thereby to have a better world. And making a difference and leaving a legacy is important to me.

And so I want *as many* people as possible to be able to enjoy the *security* and *satisfaction* that's made possible by bringing Leadsol-ogy® to life.

And that's why I created the Leadsology® Program: so I can make it affordable for YOU to benefit. And I've recently added cash flow payment options to make it even more affordable.

Please note that the Leadsology® Program is not open all of the time. Once we have a full program we close if off so we can support the people who are on the Leadsology® journey.

Visit my website at **www.leadsology.guru** and if the program is not currently open then please leave your contact details and we'll get back to you when it re-opens.

And if it is open then sign up and I'll look forward to meeting you personally online at our Q&A Coaching Call webinars and working with you step by step to bring the magic of Leadsology® to life, in *your* life!

ABOUT THE AUTHOR

Tom is a 59 year old serial entrepreneur who started his first business at age 24 and has gone on to start and sell four others, taking two of them international. In that time he's managed teams of over 100 people and annual revenue of more than 20 million.

Since 1995 Tom has dedicated himself as a full time professional to helping business owners to live a fulfilling personal and professional life whilst adding value to their clients and their own business.

At last count Tom's programs have helped well over 2,000 business owners globally across 193 different industries to develop and grow their businesses. Many have gone on to add millions to their earnings and testimonials are viewable on his website and in the last part of this book.

Tom is a previously published author and has had his writings reprinted physically in 27 countries. He's also shared international speaking platforms with the likes of Michael Gerber of E-Myth fame, Richard Koch from the 80-20 Principle, Brian Tracey and many others.

On a personal note, Tom's a New Zealander who many years ago moved to the Sunshine Coast of Queensland, Australia, which is also where he met his German wife. Locally they're known as "the Kiwi and the Kraut".

Tom and his wife have separate businesses but they work and live together in an idyllic setting next to the beach with their Border Collie dog, Monty. They have seven children and seven grand-children and Tom says he loves them all dearly and that he's equally joyous that none of them live with him anymore.

Made in the USA
Coppell, TX
30 June 2020

29812090R00134